1975

This book may be kept

FOURTEE

Twayne's United States Authors Series

Sylvia E. Bowman, *Editor*

INDIANA UNIVERSITY

Margaret Ayer Barnes

Margaret Ayer Barnes

By LLOYD C. TAYLOR, JR.

Texas A & M University

 231

Twayne Publishers, Inc. :: New York

Library of Congress Cataloging in Publication Data

Taylor, Lloyd C   1923–
    Margaret Ayer Barnes.

    (Twayne's United States authors series, TUSAS231)
    Bibliography: p.
    1. Barnes, Margaret (Ayer) 1886–1967.
PS3503.A5722Z9   813'.5'2   73-15837
ISBN 0-8057-0037-4

For

M. E. T.

AND

A. E. W.

A. G. E.

E. T. L.

ALL OF WHOM HAVE LIVED YEARS OF GRACE

Preface

In 1930 Margaret Ayer Barnes at the age of forty-four blazed somewhat meteorically across the American literary horizon with the publication of her first novel, *Years of Grace,* which won her the Pulitzer Prize the following year. However, thirty years later, her fiction, for the most part, lies unread on library shelves. When her novels first appeared, they usually found their way to the "best seller" and "recommended reading" lists; and she has retained her reputation of being "a good storyteller." In current literary histories one would be hard pressed to discover anything more than a fleeting reference to her; yet, unlike many popular authors, she consistently drew a favorable critical response.

The contemporary neglect of Mrs. Barnes is a fate which she shares generally with many other literary figures who have been dismissed because of intense concentration upon the giants of the moment. Perhaps a more explicit reason for her failure to retain the interest of the reading public and to attract the attention of the literary historian is the narrow scope of her work. All of her fiction centers on the upper middle class in America during the forty-year span from the 1890's through the 1930's. Furthermore, the fact that she chose Chicago as the principal locale for most of her novels has caused her to be classified as a regionalist which makes her work seem still more limited.[1]

It is difficult to conceive of Margaret Barnes as a regionalist in the usual sense of that designation. Neither the city of Chicago in particular nor the area of the Middle West in general plays any significant role in her work, as it does, for example, in many of the writers of the Chicago Renaissance. From her characters and her detailed description of their environment, one can envision them in a drawing room in New York as readily as in one in Chicago; for Mrs. Barnes's interest was in the portrayal of a social class as a whole. She used a fictional approach to write a social history of the upper middle class in America during that important period of transition from the

Preface

Spanish-American War through the Great Depression; and few writers have presented such an exhaustive, dispassionate critique of the attitudes and the way of life of that socioeconomic group during these vital years of change.

One could consider also that Mrs. Barnes's fiction has fallen prey to the spirit of the times. Today there is little or no interest in the problems of the upper middle class; therefore, it is easy to dismiss an author in the "genteel tradition," and especially one who is not a satirist. The novels from the era of the 1930's that still win critical acclaim often have strong sociopolitical overtones. Although the work of Margaret Barnes sometimes fits into the category of social protest and always must be judged as social commentary, it is a far cry from the viewpoint of the social critics, such as that of John Dos Passos or that of John Steinbeck, whose fiction has endured.

A recent assessment of the total literary achievement of Mrs. Barnes pronounced that she depicted people and places with minute accuracy but expounded "a definite conservative creed."[2] A more lengthy, contemporary evaluation of *Years of Grace* concluded: "Thus *Years of Grace*, with all its moralizing, turns out to be another tract on economics. Instead of advocating 'up and doing,' however, it invites the reader to admire the cozy advantages of having led a dull, safe life and arriving at old age with a comfortably fat bank account and well-furnished house."[3]

These two judgments raise immediate objections. It is difficult to view Mrs. Barnes as a proponent of conservatism when she developed variations on the theme of feminism in all of her fiction and admired Franklin Roosevelt and the early New Deal.[4] It is equally questionable whether *Years of Grace* can be described as a trite economic treatise when another critic recently recommended it as one of the fifty novels of the twentieth century that provides a stimulating reading experience.[5]

The basis for this full-length study of Margaret Ayer Barnes is the belief that her fiction vividly re-creates one segment of the social scene of late nineteenth- and early twentieth-century America. In this respect, one critic thought she displayed much the same ability to bring the past wonderfully alive as had Frederick Lewis Allen.[6] Her novels offer, therefore, an invaluable source for the student of American social history.

In the final analysis, Mrs. Barnes's reputation will rest upon her accomplishment as a social historian rather than as a literary artist. This statement does not suggest that she did not write fluent, lucid prose; but it does mean that she made no experimental contributions in style and that her writing has none of the presently popular symbolic or poetic quality. The special talent of Mrs. Barnes rests in her ability to capture the spirit of the historical periods about which she wrote through fine description and keen characterization. Margaret Barnes herself set the creation of social history as the goal of her fiction. She believed:

In the best sense of the word . . . fiction dealing with the contemporary scene is "period fiction." When well-written, it is authentic and will become historical: a page torn authoritatively from the book of the past. The writer knows what he is talking about, which is the first great asset of any chronicler. If he is observant and conscientious, he will tell the truth. Great Art is, after all, only truth-telling. It is the honest re-creation of life as the artist sees it. And the fact that it is *seen,* that in fiction it is coloured and enriched by the point of view of the author, gives a note of passionate and imaginative conviction to the portrayal that is lacking in the colder representation of biography or history. . . . In the end, it is fiction that preserves for posterity the temper of an age.[7]

Margaret Ayer Barnes succeeded admirably in her chosen literary field as an American chronicler. A close reading of her novels gives a firmer understanding of the American experience during the modern era. But, more specifically, the interested reader discovers illuminating insight into two increasingly important, contemporary issues: the course of feminism and the challenge to the leadership of the establishment.

Perhaps a word is needed to explain the reason for the liberal number of quotations from Mrs. Barnes's work. Since her fiction is not widely known today, it is hoped that by giving varied examples of her subtle use of dialogue and excellent sense of description it will encourage the unfamiliar reader to read her fiction itself rather than just to read about it.

LLOYD C. TAYLOR, JR.

Texas A & M University

Acknowledgments

I am most grateful to Houghton Mifflin Company for permission to quote from all the books of Margaret Ayer Barnes and to the Fund for Organized Research of Texas A & M University for a summer research grant.

Also I would like to express my thanks to Mrs. Wyndham B. Blanton and to Mrs. John Mc V. Haight, Jr., for sharing with me their impressions of Mrs. Barnes and her work. Mrs. Barnes graciously consented to discuss this study with me; but unfortunately her failing health never permitted it.

Mrs. Samuel C. Spangler typed the manuscript. However, she did much more than that, for her sense of humor, her enthusiasm for the subject, and her critical comments helped me over many a hurdle.

Last, but certainly not least, I am indebted to Professor Sylvia E. Bowman of Indiana University for her fine editorial criticism which proved an invaluable aid.

Finally, any errors in judgment or in fact are entirely my own.

Contents

Chronology

1886   Margaret Ayer born April 8, 1886, at Chicago, Illinois.

1904   Entered Bryn Mawr College.

1907   Graduated from Bryn Mawr with a Bachelor of Arts in English and philosophy.

1910   Married Cecil Barnes on May 21, 1910.

1912   Birth of Cecil Barnes, Jr.

1915   Birth of Edward Larrabee Barnes.

1919   Birth of Benjamin Ayer Barnes.

1920   Alumna director of Bryn Mawr.

1925   Automobile accident in France; during convalescence, began to write for her own amusement.

1926   First short stories accepted by the *Pictorial Review*.

1928   Production of *Age of Innocence*, her dramatization of Edith Wharton's novel. Publication of *Prevailing Winds*.

1929   Collaborated with Edward Sheldon on *Jenny*.

1930   Collaborated with Edward Sheldon on *Dishonored Lady*. Publication of *Years of Grace*.

1931   Received Pulitzer Prize for *Years of Grace*. Awarded an honorary Master of Arts degree by Tufts University. Publication of *Westward Passage*.

1933   *Within This Present*.

1935   *Edna His Wife*.

1936   Awarded an honorary Doctor of Literature degree by Oglethorpe University.

1938   *Wisdom's Gate*.

1967   Died at Cambridge, Massachusetts, on October 25, 1967.

The Beginning

I *A Chicago Girlhood*

THE world into which Margaret Ayer Barnes was born on
April 8, 1886, in Chicago, Illinois, epitomized cultured
gentility. Her father Benjamin F. Ayer was a distinguished,
successful lawyer and a public-spirited citizen. A graduate
of Dartmouth and the Harvard Law School, he began his legal
practice at Manchester, New Hampshire, and served one term
in the state legislature before migrating to Chicago in 1857.
Her mother was Janet Hopkins Ayer, the intellectual daughter
of Judge James Hopkins of Madison, Wisconsin, and professor
at the University of Wisconsin Law School.

In the comfortable, well-bred atmosphere, lively discussions
of current issues and ideas played a leading role in the family
life. Both parents took a keen interest in civic affairs, so the
children heard much thoughtful, spirited conversation about
the social problems and the political questions of the day. As
the youngest of five children and by temperament highly
competitive, witty, and intellectual, young Margaret Ayer thrived
on the vigorous debates with her two older brothers and sisters
as well as with her classmates at the University School for Girls.

The Ayer family, like many other prominent Chicagoans,
chose Lake Geneva, Wisconsin, for their summer residence.
Here Margaret Ayer came to know Edward Sheldon, the
future playwright and a member of a wealthy Chicago family.
They shared a passion for the theater and loved reading and
discussing the literary merits of plays as much as seeing them
performed. Many an hour they passed together under an old
apple tree by the lakeshore in rapt conversation about Rostand's

L'Aiglon and the work of other late nineteenth-century French dramatists who were their special favorites.[1]

Their friendship flourished during Sheldon's boarding-school and his college years at The Hill School and Harvard, respectively. As Margaret matured into a clever, handsome woman, he found her a delightful partner at the cotillions and at the dinner dances that sparked Chicago society during the holiday seasons. When Sheldon went to New York to begin his career as a playwright, they saw little of each other. However, after their close relationship resumed years later, it had the important result of launching her literary work.

II   *Bryn Mawr College*

After she had been graduated from the University School for Girls in 1904, she broke with prescribed tradition by choosing to attend Bryn Mawr instead of an Eastern finishing school followed by a debut. Mrs. Barnes always considered her Bryn Mawr years as one of the very vital experiences of her life.[2] From the moment she arrived at the lovely Pennsylvania campus in the autumn of 1904, she became an outstanding member of her class. One classmate remembered that Margaret Ayer, at the Freshman Rush Night, "out-shouted and out-pushed all around her, friend or foe."[3] Whenever the class of 1907 required a song for a special occasion or needed a representative to speak at a college function, it turned to Margaret Ayer.

As much as she enjoyed the fellowship and the extracurricular activities, she never permitted them to overshadow her academic work. Bryn Mawr under the dynamic leadership of President M. Carey Thomas demanded the highest scholarly achievement; for Miss Thomas, an outspoken feminist, believed fervently in the development of the professional woman. She never opposed marriage; but she insisted that a Bryn Mawr graduate, because of her superior intellect and superior training, had an obligation to participate in public life. While Margaret Ayer's intellectual interests centered on literature and philosophy, perhaps the most enduring aspect of her college education sprang from the clarion challenge of M. Carey Thomas which inspired her to write some of the most perceptive critiques of modern feminism.

III   *Return to Chicago and Marriage*

After graduation from Bryn Mawr in 1907, Margaret Ayer returned to Chicago. Many years later she described herself as "that hybrid creature,"[4] and she might well have used this description to characterize herself during the three years immediately following college. An excellent conversationalist and very energetic, she combined unusual charm with a high intelligence. She seemed to have had no special vocational inclination; yet she had no desire to conform to the traditional social pattern, for the life of the socialite bored her always. Possibly she, like many of her heroines, sought the means to bridge the gap between the world of Bryn Mawr and that of Chicago society. If she questioned her future course, she discovered the answer in her marriage on May 21, 1910, to Cecil Barnes, a native Chicagoan and a lawyer who did his undergraduate work at Harvard and who received his law degree from the Northwestern Law School.

The birth of three sons, Cecil, Jr., in 1912; Edward Larrabee in 1915; and Benjamin Ayer in 1919 added new dimensions to her life. The family spent the summers on Mount Desert Island, Maine, where she delighted in swimming, hiking, and the outdoors in general. But Margaret Barnes never allowed her domestic responsibilities to occupy her completely. Throughout her early married life she continued to develop her artistic and literary interests. Her particular cause, although it would be a term to which she would probably have objected, was higher education for women. As her sons grew up and went off to boarding school at Milton Academy in Massachusetts and then to Harvard, the range of Margaret Barnes's activities broadened.

The theater, since those summer days at Lake Geneva with Edward Sheldon, held great fascination for her. She appeared regularly in performances of the Aldis Players in Lake Forest and of the North Shore Theater in Winnetka. Also she worked enthusiastically for the Bryn Mawr Alumnae Association, always prepared to take on any job requested of her. She served as vice-president of the association, and she was elected in 1920 to a three-year term as alumna director of the college.

During her tenure as alumna director, she assisted in the establishment of the unique experiment of the Bryn Mawr

Working Woman's College initiated in the summer of 1921 by Dean Hilda Smith, a Bryn Mawr graduate and a pioneer in worker education. The idea of the two months' program grew from M. Carey Thomas's belief that the women's colleges could render significant aid in the alleviation of the industrial strife that plagued America in the aftermath of World War I. Mrs. Barnes served on the Joint Administrative Committee, which included representatives of the faculty and alumnae as well as women in industry chosen by Mary Anderson, the head of the Women's Bureau of the Department of Labor.[5]

The Joint Administrative Committee agreed upon the need for the establishment of extremely broad guidelines for admission. Their requirements consisted of a reading and writing knowledge of English, a grammar-school education or the equivalent, and a certificate of good health. They defined the working woman to be one who worked with machinery or on the assembly line, which disqualified automatically anyone who held a supervisory or clerical position. To finance the project, the committee organized teams of college women and women workers to raise scholarships of two hundred dollars each in order to meet the full expense for tuition and room and board.

Out of the two hundred and twelve applicants, the committee selected eighty for admission; and it designed the curriculum with the dual purpose of broadening individual interests and of providing deeper insight into special labor questions. The course offerings comprised: English literature and composition, labor economics, social and political history, music, and a series of special lectures on industrial organization, the role of women in the labor movement and in community life. The students could also elect instruction in baseball, swimming, tennis, and folk dancing.

The tremendous enthusiasm and the intellectual astuteness of the students may well have surprised some of the members of the Joint Administrative Committee. Although many of the women had left school at the age of twelve or thirteen, they delighted in their classes. The students on their own initiative arranged for open debates on current topics like the advantages of the trade union versus the company union, Irish independence, and legislation needed for women. If the committee had any reservations about the program at the outset, it had none when it had concluded. The members all pronounced the program to be an unqualified success and made plans to continue it in the summer of 1922. Ultimately, they realized they had inaugurated a new era in adult education in the United States; for the women who attended the Bryn Mawr summer sessions returned to their communities determined to provide more educational opportunities for themselves and others. Working in conjunction with groups like the Young Women's Christian Association, they used their Bryn Mawr experience as the blueprint to draft similar projects throughout the nation. Feminist leaders like Jane Addams, Lillian Wald, and Eleanor Roosevelt gave such projects strong support; and these programs proved a landmark in the American labor movement by training much of its future leadership.[6]

The position of alumna director entailed a certain number of speaking engagements, and Margaret Barnes distinguished herself upon the platform. Her eloquence and wit proved an invaluable aid when she headed the Chicago drive in the national campaign to raise funds for faculty salaries in 1920. More and more Bryn Mawr officials called upon her as a speaker, and she soon enlarged her scope to address civic groups and women's clubs on such subjects as the importance of higher education for women and the role of the college woman in modern society. One observer considered she possessed "a breezy sort of poise, an enormous sense of fun, a strong social intuition, an American flair for organization and work, and a charm that shines equally on beggars, kings, millionaires and book-reviewers."[7] Indeed, Mrs. Barnes might have found in lecturing the vocation she discovered in writing if fate had not intervened in the summer of 1925.

IV *A Literary Career*

In the summer of 1925 the Barnes vacationed in Europe. They joined some friends for a tour of the French cathedral towns. As their French chauffeur drove onto the highway outside of Rouen, their limousine met another car in a head-on collision. Margaret Barnes fractured her skull, her back, and three ribs. "For a long time, I was nothing but bandages and plaster casts and odd, unpleasant colors," she recalled. "As I became better, I needed some sedentary occupation and started writing short stories just for the pleasure I could get from it. I held the paper above the casts covering my chest and slowly penciled the outlines of some incidents and people who had interested me."[8]

After many weeks in the American Hospital in Paris, her physicians agreed to permit her to return to Chicago for additional treatment. Her back continued to cause her excruciating pain, and medical opinion held that she would have to resign herself to the fact that she would be at least partially bedridden. She accepted the pain, but she fought against invalidism as long as there remained the faintest glimmer of hope for more recovery. When in March, 1926, she journeyed to New York for a consultation with Dr. Russell Hibbs of the New York Orthopedic Hospital, his examination lifted her morale tremendously. He believed another operation on her back could improve her condition; however, he emphasized that it would entail a long convalescence strapped to a spinal board, and he warned that he could not guarantee complete recovery, only improvement. Mrs. Barnes never hesitated. Her high courage and her sense of humor carried her triumphantly through the ordeal of surgery.

Her difficult, painful convalescence was brightened by the resumption of her close friendship with Edward Sheldon, also a patient of Dr. Hibbs. Sheldon, now totally disabled by arthritis and soon to lose his eyesight but never his heroic spirit, made her his special concern. Understanding only too well the monotony of the hospital routine, the popular playwright flooded her with reading material from the novels of Henry James to the latest issue of the *Police Gazette*. He broke the tedium of hospital food with surprise presents of special soups and liqueurs. Once he ordered a huge assortment of colored balloons to decorate the ceiling of her room. A steady exchange of telephone calls and notes showed them that the intervening years had not drawn them apart.[9]

One morning Sheldon prepared a list of mutual Chicago friends with whom he had lost touch and asked her to write a comment on each of them. He originally had no motive except occupational therapy; but her incisive analyses so impressed him that he telephoned her at once that she must begin work on a short story. His advice pleased her immensely, so she began in earnest to revise her earlier efforts and to compose new ones, all of which won Sheldon's enthusiastic approval. By the time she had attained out-patient status, she had completed several short stories. Armed with a crutch and a cane she made her way to the office of the *Pictorial Review* whose editor, a friend of Sheldon, immediately accepted her work.

During her final weeks in New York, Margaret Barnes visited the playwright frequently. Upon the occasion of their first dinner together, he proposed that she should dramatize his friend Edith Wharton's *Age of Innocence*. "I don't know just how seriously he himself took the venture at first," she explained. "He persuaded me to try to write the play, and then we talked over the construction in detail. Then I went back to Chicago."[10]

V *The Making of a Playwright*

Once removed from the contagious enthusiasm of Sheldon, Mrs. Barnes developed grave reservations about her ability as a dramatist. Her own experience in the theater had made her aware of the practical problems involved in writing a good play, and she understood intuitively the dangerous pitfalls that confronted the playwright in the preparation of an acclaimed novel for the stage. She admitted that the whole idea of the project fascinated her; yet she questioned whether she could execute it successfully. It took many telephone conversations and telegrams of encouragement from Sheldon before she mustered the self-confidence to mail the first act to him. He replied with the announcement that he had cabled Edith Wharton for the dramatic rights.

Now Mrs. Barnes worked at fever pitch; however, the nagging doubt about her competence persisted. Before she had finished the final draft, Sheldon submitted it to Guthrie McClintic for Katherine Cornell's consideration. The actress accepted the role of Ellen Olenska without waiting to read the completed version. Margaret Barnes insisted that Sheldon should be listed as co-author; but he countered her every argument. Nevertheless, she always acknowledged her debt to him and never ceased to state publicly that she owed her literary career to him. Reviewing one of the pre-Broadway performances in Baltimore, the critic wrote that he sensed the skilled hand of Sheldon throughout much of the drama. Margaret Barnes replied: "That bright boy is wasted in dramatic criticism he ought to buy himself a pair of rubber shoes and sign up with a Pinkerton agency."[11] She expressed her gratitude to Sheldon by dedicating her fourth novel *Edna His Wife* to him.

VI   Age of Innocence

Although Margaret Barnes in her dramatization followed Mrs. Wharton's novel closely, she made important alterations in the characterizations of Newland Archer and Julius Beaufort, the two men who fall in love with Countess Ellen Olenska upon her return to her native New York after she leaves her philandering husband; and she also made Countess Olenska the mistress of Archer.

Margaret Barnes strengthened the character of conventional, aristocratic Archer by portraying him as a colorful adventurer who left the constrained society of old New York to fight with Custer in the Indian wars in the West, then to return to New York to enter the political arena to lead the fight against Boss William Marcy Tweed and Tammany Hall, and to be elected to the Senate. She patterned her hero somewhat upon the career of her grandfather John Brown Ayer who had broken the Tweed Ring and upon that of Theodore Roosevelt for whom she had campaigned in the election of 1912.[12]

At first, the change incensed Mrs. Wharton, for she regarded all reformers as crude provincials. Mrs. Barnes discussed the matter at length with Mrs. Cadwalader Jones, the sister-in-law of Edith Wharton and a great friend of Sheldon. As Margaret Barnes reported her conversation to him,

Mrs. Jones and Mrs. Wharton felt absolutely . . . that a genteel young man could not dabble in politics. She [Mrs. Jones] said, "Edith thought he would not have been so vulgar," meaning so vulgar as to have fought Tweed. And they also thought it would have been a bit common to join up with Custer to fight Indians. They feel a U.S. Senator is "very distinguished" so the political career can be left in—just the mud and sweat toned down a bit. Mrs. Jones asked very sweetly, "Why would Archer have gone to a fireman's ball? It makes him seem very provincial, my dear, to be a crusader. One of the points of the book was that he was very conventional." Mrs. Jones said it nearly killed Mrs. Wharton to have us say that Archer had never been abroad—but they will compromise on a grand tour of Europe *before* the opening of the play. She didn't comment on Ellen's fall from virtue. The chastity of the heroine sinks to complete unimportance compared with the gentility of the hero! It is apparently immaterial whether or not Archer spends the night with Ellen so long as he doesn't go to the fireman's ball. Our Archer appears a monstrous changeling in the cradle of Mrs. Wharton's hero![13]

However, in the end, the playwright smoothed the ruffled feelings of the novelist; and Edith Wharton wrote warmly to Sheldon about the high literary quality of the adaptation.

If Mrs. Wharton did not care for the treatment of Archer, she made no recorded comment about the interpretation of Beaufort. In the novel, Julius Beaufort is depicted as a lecherous, scheming parvenu who cleverly exploits a knowledge of the arts to pass himself off as a cultivated gentleman. Margaret Barnes, while retaining the general outline of the character, presented him as a sophisticated intellectual whose unscrupulousness grows as a defense mechanism against a society that accepts his wealth and the pleasures it can offer but rejects him as an individual because of his lowly origin.

As Mrs. Barnes knew only too well, she could not have chosen a more formidable task for her first theatrical venture than the dramatization of a popular novel by a celebrated author. To retain the flavor of the original and at the same time to make changes and deletions that will enhance the dramatic impact require craftsmanship which a neophyte writer seldom possesses. However, she succeeded where many more experienced authors had failed. For, as one critic judged, "Nothing in the theater is more hazardous than fashioning a play from a novel, and the process is especially fraught with peril when the book is so completely a study and a narrative as Mrs. Wharton's *The Age of Innocence*. But Mrs. Barnes, with the intrepidity of an accomplished tyro, has managed to compress the characters and events of this expansive story of old New York into a competent stage tale, and to distill its lavender essences in a manner that should be gratifying even to its

fastidious author."[14] The general critical assessment was that
"Mrs. Barnes had skillfully, almost uncannily, avoided the
dangers which beset adapters," for the drama itself "does
capture some of the charm of Mrs. Wharton's novel, does somehow evoke the feeling of time and place and make them glamorous and touching."[15]

VII *Collaboration with Edward Sheldon*

Edward Sheldon not only took great pleasure in his protégée's
achievement but found her so delightful as a person that he
suggested that they collaborate officially on a play. Their first
joint effort resulted in *Jenny*, a light, sophisticated comedy
about the love affair of an actress and a middle-aged businessman. The play proved an acceptable, if not especially exciting,
vehicle for Jane Cowl and Sir Guy Standing for the Broadway
season of 1929. However, before they had completed *Jenny*,
the playwrights began to discuss some ideas for a murder drama.
Sheldon had become increasingly addicted to criminal studies;
and, before *Jenny* went into rehearsal, they had selected their
next plot from the sensational British trial in 1857 of Madeleine
Smith, the member of a prominent Scotch family who had
murdered her French lover when he had threatened to divulge
their affair to her fiancé.

While the Smith trial inspired the idea for *Dishonored Lady*,
Mrs. Barnes and Sheldon used it more as a skeletal basis than
anything else: they updated it to contemporary New York, so
the heroine became a wealthy socialite and her lover a nightclub
entertainer. *Dishonored Lady* is certainly highly melodramatic;
yet it does have an impact. In part, this comes from the
characterization of the heroine Madeleine Grey, a lovely, cultured aristocrat who becomes a murderess. However, more
important is the frank treatment of sex by the playwrights,
although it seems very mild when judged by today's standards.
A passionate, realistic love scene precedes the murder, a
sequence which creates a particularly grisly effect. A number
of leading actresses, including Ethel Barrymore, the dramatists'
first choice, refused to accept a role in the play because of the
sexual realism. When the drama opened in 1930 with Katherine

Cornell in the lead, it was one of the hits and sensations of the season.

As sensational as the play itself was the plagiarism suit filed by Mrs. Barnes and Sheldon against Metro-Goldwyn-Mayer. Shortly after the premiere of *Dishonored Lady*, the motion-picture company had sought the film rights; and the playwrights had rewritten the scenario several times in an attempt to produce one that would meet the approval of the Hays Office. After a year of fruitless effort, the negotiations had ended. Meanwhile, Mrs. Belloc Lowndes, the British novelist, published her novel *Letty Lynton*, also based on the Madeleine Smith trial; and Metro-Goldwyn-Mayer purchased the rights to Mrs. Lowndes's book. But, in the movie version of *Letty Lynton*, the company incorporated copyrighted material from *Dishonored Lady* without permission. The case, which went to court in April, 1933, took seven years to settle. Finally in 1940, the Supreme Court upheld the playwrights' plea and ordered Metro-Goldwyn-Mayer to pay damages in excess of one-half million dollars, one of the largest settlements ever awarded in a plagiarism suit.[16]

If the collaboration with Sheldon established the literary ability of Mrs. Barnes, it proved to be of tremendous importance to him. He had feared that his crippling, physical invalidism had also destroyed his creativity; but his work with Margaret Barnes convinced him that his illness had in no way damaged his creative vision. Although he did not do any actual writing himself after 1930, he embarked on a new career of acting as a consultant to playwrights and actors. It would be impossible to gauge his influence because he insisted upon complete anonymity; however, it would be safe to say that, from 1930 until his death in 1946, at least one production and one performance of every Broadway season owed its success and critical acclaim to Sheldon's advice.[17]

VII *The Turn toward Fiction*

While it would be impossible to overemphasize the role of Edward Sheldon in the launching of Margaret Barnes's career as a writer, she probably chose to concentrate more heavily upon building her reputation as a novelist as a result of the influence of her sister Janet Ayer Fairbank. Mrs. Fairbank published her first novel, *At Home,* in 1910; but, at this time, politics began to dominate her activity. She became a leader in the woman's suffrage movement and an enthusiastic supporter of Theodore Roosevelt. In 1912 she headed the Western division of the Progressive party. During World War I, she served on the Council of National Defense; and in 1919 she became a member of the executive committee of the Democratic party. Although she continued her political work, she resumed her literary career with the publication of her second novel, *The Cortlandts of Washington Square,* in 1923.

Margaret Barnes followed closely the public life of her sister, but she showed no desire to participate actively. Nevertheless, Progressivism contributed markedly toward the shaping of her social philosophy; for she remained a firm advocate of feminism, humanitarianism, and pacifism. From the very few direct political allusions in her fiction, she seemingly was an admirer of Robert La Follette. Therefore, considering the closeness of the sisters and of their ideas and interests, Janet Fairbank's writing again seriously may very well have turned the younger sister's thought in that direction. In the dedication of her second novel, *Westward Passage,* Mrs. Barnes wrote: "To J. A. F. Who Blazed the Trail."[18] In any event, Margaret Barnes collected the short stories she had written during her convalescence and in 1928 published them in the volume *Prevailing Winds.* When *Dishonored Lady* went into production in 1930, she had finished her first novel. Henceforth, she sought to achieve her mark as a writer of fiction.

CHAPTER 2

Prevailing Winds

M<small>RS.</small> BARNES noted in the preface to the second edition of *Prevailing Winds* that the stories represented her first attempt "to re-create in written words the conclusions I had drawn from life itself."[1] In "Feather Beds," "The Dinner Party," "Arms and the Boy," and "Perpetual Care," she drew subtle sketches of the American character and social attitudes.[2]

I *"Feather Beds"*

At first glance, "Feather Beds" seems only an amusing trifle about a weekend house party on the Long Island estate of Ethel and Matthew Martin to entertain Susy and Chuck Dayton with whom Matthew grew up in Connersville, Indiana, and whom Ethel happened to meet on a Santa Barbara vacation. Unknown to Ethel, Susy and Matthew had been secretly engaged before they had decided they preferred money to love. Matthew had attended the Columbia University Medical School and, after a brilliant record, embarked on a career in cancer research at the Pierrepont Institute founded by Ethel's father. A combination of ability and ambition established him as a leading young luminary in the medical world, and marriage to the lovely and fashionable Ethel Pierrepont brought him wealth and social position. Meanwhile, Susy, the prettiest girl in Connersville, had married Chuck, the son of the town's wealthiest citizen. After much vacillation between the choice of a career in the theater or one in the church, Chuck became an Episcopal clergyman. His extreme good looks, his suavity of manner, and his chic wife had won him a California bishopric.

At the outset, only Matthew experiences any apprehension

about the weekend. He views the situation as "Just the sort of thing that happened in bad novels and successful plays and, yes, possibly in day-dreams, but never in real life."[3] His sense of foreboding heightens when he learns that the trustees of the Pierrepont Institute have selected this particular weekend to consider the appointment of the new director, the goal upon which Matthew has set his sights.

In this skillful charade, Margaret Barnes, through the characterizations of Chuck and Matthew, underscored the shallowness of the professional man. She described the entrance of the Bishop: "Chuck descended, picturesquely clerical in his sable waistcoat. His gaitered legs tripped nimbly down the stairs. No spoil-sport, Chuck. A regular fellow. The hand adorned with the Episcopal ring accepted a second cocktail with benevolent alacrity. Even before the announcement of dinner, it was clear he was intriguing Jocelyn [another guest]. Her little mocking face was eager as she looked up into his earnest eyes. His head was bent in a pleasing mixture of flattery and benediction" (66–67). Chuck delights in the pulpit like the actor who loves the stage because it thrills his ego to see the audience captivated by his personal appeal. The caliber and depth of the performance mean nothing to Chuck.

Matthew in an entirely different way reflects the same irresponsible vanity. After dinner, while the others settle down to bridge, Matthew and Susy stroll in the garden. The garden, perfect in every detail and very romantic in the moonlight, reminds her of the perfection and romance of their lives; for, as she explains to him, they both have obtained what they had sought years ago in Connersville. When Matthew retorts that purpose and romance disappeared from his life when they broke their engagement, Susy replies lightly:

> "This talk is—foolish. We made beds—"
> "And now we lie in them."
> "They're feather beds," said Susy brightly.
> "That's something anyway." (76)

Refusing to renounce his illusion of broken romance, Matthew by the end of the visit convinces Susy to elope with him. They will flee to Vienna where he will conquer even more brilliant medical horizons with her as his inspiration. However, alone in his bedroom, his sense of realism challenges his romantic vision. He spends a sleepless night weighing the desirability of impecunious Susy against that of affluent Ethel.

When Matthew arrives the next morning at the breakfast table, he finds two telegrams at his place. The first one he opens announces his appointment as director of the Pierrepont Institute, and all thought of Susy and elopement vanish. So absorbed is he with himself that he never notices the absence of the Daytons until another guest comments upon it. When Ethel answers that they had taken an early train so that Susy would have more time to shop in New York, Matthew seems dumfounded; then he remembers the other telegram. Signed by Susy, it reads: "Can you ever forgive me? For being a coward?" (92). As Matthew's eyes wander from the telegram to the view of the perfect garden through the dining room window, he suddenly realizes:

Why—he had kept everything. Even Susy's illusions. He must send her a beautiful telegram. There was only one Susy. But—could he ever forgive her?
Well, frankly, he could. (92–93)

II   "The Dinner Party"

More substantial and more searching than "Feather Beds" is "The Dinner Party," which concerns one evening in the life of Martha Cavendish, a Bryn Mawr graduate, the socially prominent wife of successful and popular Tommy, and the mother of three children. Despite her genuinely happy married life, she has never fully reconciled the goals instilled in her at college with her comfortable, pleasant, but rather aimless existence as a Chicago society woman. At a dinner party of familiar guests, she discovers an unexpected surprise in the presence of Hugh Cameron, now an internationally famous artist, whom she had loved at seventeen. Their youthful romance had faded when he had gone abroad to study and when she had gone to Bryn Mawr. This meeting causes Martha to ponder how differently time has dealt with each of them.

Hugh, she feels, has grown admirably. Having begun his

career as a fashionable portrait painter, he had tired of a dilettante reputation and had developed into a serious artist. She, on the other hand, after the intellectual stimulus of Bryn Mawr, had settled for the conventional role of a proper marriage. Even participation in civic affairs has not attracted her, for she concludes uncertainly: "These earnest women with causes—funny to her there was something so frivolous about them fundamentally. They took their ... [causes] with such child-like solemnity, and yet wasn't the stir somehow all on the surface? Or was it just her own limitation that she couldn't conceive of a cause about which *she* could really be earnest, as she conceived of earnestness?" (178). Since she has no inclination for the life of action, she has substituted for it the life of contemplation. To try to understand the motives of men and to gain insights into the nature of human existence seem more vital to her than heading committees or launching drives. Yet Martha cannot escape the feeling that she is only indulging in rationalization.

Hugh jolts her from her reverie with the suggestion of a walk on the terrace. Alone together, time evaporates. When he confesses that he has never understood why their romance had failed, Martha answers: "Just life—and youth. The young are so helpless and so pathetically docile. They think the world is their oyster. But circumstances conquer them. They don't know, yet, that they can surmount that. Distance, you know, and time, and incident. And then, of course, they don't know how precious a thing they have to lose. Until it's gone. It was just . . . Europe for you; Chicago for me" (200).

Hugh dismisses her explanation as too prosaic, for he cannot believe she has found real happiness with Tommy in Chicago. He exclaims: "Don't you see? Don't you realize? How you're wasted? Just as an audience, no matter how discerning? You're far too precious, can't you understand, just to applaud the play!" (202). When he has finished speaking, Martha rises to her feet a little unsteadily and answers him: "Hugh, dear, don't. You said it all before nineteen years ago, under this very clematis" (203). Before he can make any reply, the rest of the dinner party engulfs them.

As Martha leaves with Tommy, Hugh follows them to their car. Waiting for Tommy to take his seat beside her, she turns quickly to Hugh: "Hugh . . . it's been lovely seeing you like this, talking to you, being with you again. It's been—oh, my dear, what is there to say? But I want you to understand. Really, I mean, I want you always to know" (204). When Tommy starts the engine of the car, Martha realizes her life has assumed a totality that it has never had before. She recognizes she possesses knowledge which Hugh, for all of his experience of the world, has never attained. She knows conclusively now what she has always felt: real adventure lies in the exploration of the self.

III   *"Arms and the Boy"*

Mrs. Barnes shifted her perspective somewhat in "Arms and the Boy" from the American social scene to the psychological impact of World War I, and this story represents her most skillful effort in the genre. Certainly, it deserves an audience today; for it remains an exceptionally astute, trenchant analysis of the war experience. In the story, Michael, scion of a distinguished Chicago family and a student at Princeton, falsifies his age in order to enter Officer Candidate School upon the American declaration of war. After receiving his commission, he is sent to Paris where he meets Marthe, a young prostitute who has arrived recently in the capital from the provinces to earn her living. She persuades him to take an apartment for them; and, when he is ordered to the front, she waits for him faithfully. When he is wounded and invalided back to Paris, she nurses him; and their ensuing months together convince Michael that he loves Marthe. After the Armistice, he promises her that he will return to marry her after his graduation from college. However, Marthe views their time together as a lovely interlude in their lives that has now ended.

Although Michael never doubts his love for Marthe, he finds it increasingly difficult to convey to her in his letters the undergraduate joys of Princeton. Her image blurs in the excitement of football weekends, for she had ceased to exist for him during "the glorious half-hour when he stood shouting for the touchdowns of the Tiger in the Princeton cheering section of the Yale Bowl" (236). Following his graduation from Princeton, he returns to Chicago where the dazzle of debut

balls and the thrill of being lionized as the young man-about-
town obliterates all the memories of Marthe, Paris, and the
war. He becomes engaged to Barbara, the season's most
celebrated debutante. At his wedding he recalls Marthe:

Confronted with Barbara's tender, tangible presence, the little
wistful ghost that walked the corridors of memory seemed strangely
vague and visionary. It had no place in the sweet and silly ceremony
of the wedding. In the foolish, formal fluster over ushers' neckties
and bridesmaids' bouquets. It paled before the tulle-clad vision of
a strangely chastened Barbara, standing at his side under a bell of
smilax, presenting a cool young cheek to the conventional salutation
of their little world. It shrank before the uproarious horde of young
men in cutaways, who threatened him obscurely from distant corners
with fistfuls of rice and bows of satin ribbon, and escorted the bride,
with Princeton cheers and bursts of popular melody, to cut the
monumental cake, romantically enough—the idea had been Barbara's—with his veteran's sword. (239–41)

However, as they sail for their European honeymoon, the
specter of Marthe arises once more to taunt Michael. He sees
clearly, and now he fears too late, that she had offered him
above everything else the one opportunity to break from the
constrained circle of convention which henceforth would shape
the pattern of his existence. Their arrival in Paris terrifies him,
for he fancies he sees her on every street corner. Then the
dreadful moment comes when he encounters her at Lanvin's
where he has accompanied Barbara for a fitting.

The Marthe he meets is not the girl he had abandoned. Now
the mistress of a multimillionaire nobleman, she epitomizes
chic and sophistication. Michael, overwhelmed by remorse,
blames himself for her fate. But she chides him lightly to
remember that in her way she has become a work of art. As
Marthe departs, Barbara appears:

The door to the fitting-room swung open on a reassuring vision . . .
where, framed in the crystal planes of a triple mirror, Barbara stood,
straight and slim and boyish in the crisp white folds of a taffeta
dinner gown. The blue ribbon of her girdle matched the color in
her candid eyes. The knot of rosebuds at her shoulders deepened
the flush on her rounded cheeks. Her thin arms hung awkwardly

down upon her silver flounces. Above the straight white bodice, a square of summer tan marred the childlike purity of her neck and throat. Her little freckled nose was wrinkled with her inquiring smile. (254–56)

This momentary glimpse of Barbara erases Michael's nagging doubts about himself and about the rightness of his marriage, for his wife's engaging freshness seems soothing when compared to the lacquered magnificence of Marthe. The unsettling memories of Marthe and the war vanish forever. The moments that really count, Michael reflects, are those like cheering for the Princeton team in the Yale Bowl, the lovely formality of debutante balls, or the wonderful gaiety of wedding receptions like his and Barbara's. He vows he will reverence always the immutable traditions of that little world to which he and Barbara belong; for these, he asserts, represent the vital, truly meaningful things in life.

IV "Perpetual Care"

Margaret Barnes returned to an analysis of social attitudes in "Perpetual Care." The story focuses on one memorable day in the life of Kate Dalton, a wealthy, prominent Chicago dowager of fifty-nine; and the introduction of Kate is striking:

Kate Dalton came slowly down her elliptical staircase, her slender hand clasping, just a little too carefully for comfort, the delicate iron rail. It was lovely, of course, to look at, but how disconcerting to have a staircase that always made you remember you were fifty-nine. Sooner or later she would certainly slip on those triangular treads. Slip ignominiously down at the feet of her own butler, standing with deferential dignity on the black-and-white tiles below. What would Sands do about it, she wondered, when the day came? Would he lapse, even momentarily, from the perfect manservant as he scrambled her to her feet? Appalling, really, to be fifty-nine ... appalling to fumble, be it ever so little on any staircase! Reassuring to hear her still shapely, high-heeled slippers tap briskly, competently on the marble flooors. (259)

Pausing to see that her drawing room is prepared to receive her dinner guests, she notices with delight that her reflection

in the mirror does not betray her years now that she no longer
dresses in mourning for her husband Sam. The thought of
mourning causes her to reflect:

Ridiculous, mourning. Fancy dress . . . what had two yards of
crisp black crepe, dragging her hat back and giving her a headache,
to do with the curiously disproportionate sense of desolation that
Sam's death had brought into her life. But she had never dared
to say that even to the boys, let alone to Katherine . . . whose grief
for her father seemed somehow all expended in the sacred significance
of a grosgrain ribbon, the decent distinction between a suède and a
shiny black kid glove. (259–60)

Her thoughts linger on her children. Bob, the oldest, had
been expelled from Yale but had distinguished himself at
Château-Thierry, only to end as the idol of the nightclub set
and to marry and to divorce foolish, vacuous, lovable Lily.
Chris, her other son, charming, gallant, amusing, has employed
all of his vast potential talent toward the pursuit of aimless
pleasure. Katherine, her only daughter, so fashionable, so handsome, so wealthy, has remained totally blind to the adventure
of living. None of them, she concludes, has either understood
or kept triumphantly "the rendezvous with life" (264).

The announcement of her butler of the arrival of her chauffeur
interrupts her reverie and reminds her that she has a medical
appointment that afternoon. Despite some seizures of pain, she
never anticipates the verdict which she forces out of her
physician: she has eight months to live. The recollection of her
dinner party before the performance of *La Traviata* arouses her
from her state of uncomprehending astonishment. She decides
with bravado to wear all of her jewels and to try out the new
scarlet lipstick Chris had given her for Christmas.

The intimate party consists of her children; Ida and Fred,
her closest friends who had lured Sam and her from their
native Vermont to seek their fortune in Chicago; and Raymond,
a distinguished marine biologist whom she has loved for years.
The doctor's pronouncement seems utterly fantastic in the
midst of this congenial gaiety.

Later at the opera, Kate's attention strays from the star-
crossed love of Violetta and Alfredo to that of Raymond and
her. From the moment they had acknowledged their love that

summer long ago at Woods Hole where she had been vacationing with the children and where he had been researching at the marine laboratory, they had accepted the futility of that love. Raymond understood that her sense of duty to Sam prohibited either a divorce or an affair. After Sam's death, they considered the thought of marriage ludicrous. Kate knew intuitively that he felt, as she did, that "people such as they, who had loved and lost with such tragic desperation in the early thirties, didn't marry, grotesquely at fifty-nine. Marrying absurdly, surrounded by incredulous offsprings and bouncing grandchildren. Accept as mendicants, from the condescending hands of Destiny, something so much less good than they could have taken for themselves. No, Raymond's dramatic sense of living equaled her own. For him, too, it was quite impossible, a ridiculous anti-climax to that early dream" (293–94).

The death of Violetta makes Kate wonder what deathbed she would choose. Definitely she would not have Raymond there, for she is determined to remain for him "always, the woman in the doorway, the figure on the threshold of something he could not attain" (294). More than anything else, she decides, she would like to spend the months that remained in her Vermont birthplace; to slip away now, then they would all remember her sitting in regal splendor ablaze with jewels in an opera box.

But, no, she must open the family stucco villa at Palm Beach so that Bob can have his regular month's visit with his son Robbie. Lily counted on her to see that Bob behaved himself when the boy stayed with his father. Moreover, she concludes with amusement, how horrified the children would be if she should voice her preference for the lovely Vermont hills to "the marble mausoleum in Graceland, under the shadow of the elevated railway, with the sound of the Clark Street trolley, if it were not mercifully stilled in the silence of eternity, forever in her ears" (294–95).

In the face of death as in life, Kate agrees to bow to the dictates of established social convention because she knows any other course would disturb profoundly those whom she most desires to help. Nevertheless, she realizes that she could not bring herself to accept this decision with equanimity if she had not experienced those exhilarating, dangerous moments of being "divinely a fool" (264). Now, at the end of her life, she can proclaim that she has attained "Peace, without victory" (263).

After Kate's interment in the marble mausoleum in Graceland, her children derive great consolation from the thought that at least they have given her the correct funeral that she would have wished. The perfect grooming of the cemetery impresses them. Katherine declares: "That's what you pay for. What they guarantee in their little booklet. I always like their phrase—perpetual care. And it always makes me think of Mother. Just what she gave us. You know Mother never had a thought for herself. Funny to think of anyone like Mother—never caring to have a life of her own" (296–97).

Margaret Ayer Barnes made an impressive debut with *Prevailing Winds;* but in this collection of short stories, as in her subsequent novels, there exists little variation in the theme and structure of her fiction. Her point of view is always that of a chronicler. Mrs. Barnes, who had a high regard for the short story as an art form, stated that she found their composition more difficult than the novel. There is no question that the short story as a mode of expression does not suit the presentation of her ideas as well as the novel. For example, detailed descriptions of differences in décor, manner of dress, social or educational backgrounds contribute greatly to the effectiveness of her work. Even at her best in the short story, she gives the impression of being cramped. Only "Feather Beds" is truly satisfying; and it, with the exception of the incisive characterizations of Chuck Dayton and Matthew Martin, is the least consequential of the significant stories in the collection.

In reading particularly "Arms and the Boy" and "Perpetual Care," we feel constantly that these would make wonderful novels. To echo one reviewer of *Prevailing Winds,* it is a real pity that she did not return to the story of Kate Dalton, for she sketched in "Perpetual Care" the character of a fascinating woman whose full life should have been told.[4]

However, many of the factors which contribute to the success of the novels do appear in the short stories. Mrs. Barnes displayed a fine ear for dialogue and excellent ability to develop character through nuance in conversation, an aptitude certainly sharpened by her experience as a playwright.

Equally her settings are always right, which again shows how much she had learned from the theater. Only in the case of "The Dinner Party" can there be detected any direct influence on the creation of the novels; in this instance, it could almost be said that *Years of Grace* is an outgrowth of the short story.

Despite their shortcomings, these four stories are consistently interesting and very readable; at their best, they demonstrate "a high emotional quality" because Margaret Barnes discerned with clever insight the prevailing winds of change that threatened the complacent security of the upper middle class American.[5]

CHAPTER 3

Years of Grace

A FTER the publication of *Prevailing Winds*, Margaret Barnes
concentrated on the novel. In 1930, *Years of Grace*, which
established her literary reputation and which won her the
Pulitzer Prize in 1931, presented a richly detailed study of
late nineteenth- and early twentieth-century American society.
Through the life of Jane Ward Carver, the daughter of a
prominent Chicago family, Mrs. Barnes examined the shifting
social scene from the rigid conventionality of the 1890's through
the disturbing transitional years of the Progressive Era and
World War I to the garish Jazz Age of the 1920's and the
eve of the Great Depression.

I *The World of Jane Ward*

The world of Jane Ward at seventeen is represented by the
library of her father, which she loves:

It was quite small and the walls were covered with black-walnut
bookcases with glass doors, behind which the leather-covered volumes
of her father's library glowed in subdued splendor. Over the bookcases were four steel engravings, one of George Washington and
one of Thomas Jefferson and one of Daniel Webster and one of
Abraham Lincoln—the four greatest Americans, her father always
said. On the mantelpiece was a mahogany bust of William Shake-
speare. "The Bard of Avon" was carved in a scroll on its little
pedestal. The sofa by the fire was covered in dark brown velvet
and there were two big leather chairs and a revolving one . . . behind
the big green baize-topped desk of black-walnut. Near the desk
was a globe on a black-walnut stand, with a barometer hanging
over it. That was all there was in the room except a big branch
rubber tree in one west window.[1]

Quiet gentility characterizes the adolescent world of Jane Ward. Although Jane prizes the traditional, staunchly conservative ideals of her family, she longs to experience something of the life beyond the narrow perimeter of her existence. She shows her sturdy independent spirit in her choice of friends; for, among her classmates at Miss Milgrim's School, she prefers Agnes Johnson, the clever daughter of a career woman and a liberal journalist, to Muriel Lester and Flora Furness, girls from influential families whom she has known from the cradle. But, above everything else, her youthful romance with André Duroy displays her desire to be independent in thought and in action.

André, the artistic son of the French consul and his English wife, represents an unconventional cosmopolitanism that intrigues Jane. He refuses to follow the traditional path to Harvard, Yale, or Princeton; instead, he intends to study in Europe for a career as a sculptor. When their friendship blossoms into romance and he asks her to marry him, Jane, realizing her age would prohibit marriage, hopes to strike a compromise with an engagement. However, her parents oppose her; and Mrs. Ward, who has no intention of having André for a son-in-law, insists that there is to be no communication between them until Jane is twenty-one. Sadly, she parts with André; but, at the same time, she receives some compensation by winning reluctant parental approval to enter Bryn Mawr with Agnes rather than go to Farmington with Muriel and Flora.

II *Bryn Mawr*

From Jane's first day on the campus, she loves every aspect of Bryn Mawr life. Slowly, nevertheless, it dawns on her that she does not possess the scholarly drive and intense determination for academic achievement so characteristic of her classmates. This growing awareness disturbs her, for she knows that the goal of the brilliant, dynamic President M. Carey Thomas, whom she finds personally so inspiring, is to prepare women for positions of leadership.

By the end of her sophomore year, Jane's dilemma mounts. Her mother has made it very plain that she must return to

Chicago at the end of the term to "come out" with Muriel and Flora. In part, she admits that her reluctance to leave Bryn Mawr springs from her disinterest in being a debutante; yet she also recognizes that she has absorbed some of the crusading zeal of Miss Thomas and that perhaps she might want to participate in furthering the humanitarian reforms about which Miss Thomas speaks so eloquently. At least, she knows she desires a Bryn Mawr degree. Nevertheless, she cannot bring herself to withstand the parental verdict.

III   Society, Stephen, and Marriage

During her first autumn in Chicago, Jane's thoughts center upon Bryn Mawr, and she goes in her imagination through the day-to-day college routine. Her only sustaining thought is knowing that she has only two more years to wait for André. Then, almost imperceptibly, she gets caught up in the excitement of the debut festivities. Only when she happens to glance at her college books does she suffer a pang of regret. Even the image of André dims when she meets Stephen Carver of Boston, Flora's cousin who has come to Chicago to work in the western branch of the family bank. Stephen, handsome, wealthy, and socially impeccable, falls in love with Jane. However, she refuses to consider their relationship on any basis except friendship.

At the end of the debut year, Jane faces the future uncertainly:

André—Jane knew, now, of course, that the family couldn't have let her marry at seventeen. She couldn't even imagine now, what their life would have been together, what her life would have been without all those other experiences that had crowded into it since she had closed the door on that romance. Bryn Mawr and all the things she had learned there . . . Miss Thomas, with her flaming torch of enlightenment, and that gay, carefree life in Pembroke Hall. The beauty of the Bryn Mawr countryside. This last year, too, with its funny frivolities, its social amenities, its growing friendships with people Jane knew, really, in her heart of hearts, were awfully unlike herself. All these experiences were part of her now. Inalienable. Not ever to be ignored, or belittled, or set lightly aside. (152–53)

Of these new friendships, hers with Stephen disturbs her the most profoundly. She admits readily that she finds him charming and attractive; yet she understands, too, how basically incompatible their outlooks are when they have a heated discussion on the subject of the college woman:

> "Do you know," said Stephen confidentially, "I really hate college women?"
> "I am a college woman," she said.
> "You?" Stephen burst out laughing.
> "I'm a fighting feminist," said Jane.
> "Yes, you are!" said Stephen.
> "Really I am," said Jane. "I just haven't the courage of my convictions."
> "I like you cowardly," said Stephen.
> "It has its advantages," said Jane. "She who thinks and runs away, lives to think another day . . . I don't act at all . . . I just drift." (183–84)

The combination of the declaration of the Spanish-American War and the long-awaited letter from André causes her to drift into marriage with Stephen. On the afternoon when Stephen comes to beg her for the last time to marry him before he leaves for Cuba with the Rough Riders, Janes receives André's letter, informing her that he has won the *Prix de Rome* which will require him to postpone his journey to America for another year. She, longing to end her indecision about her future, replies by announcing her engagement to Stephen. While Jane believes her engagement has settled her uncertainty about herself, her wedding day brings an upsurge of nagging doubts. She experiences "an odd sensation of playing a role" (216–17), but she reminds herself sternly: "Dear Stephen! she *did* love him. She *would* love him. She had married him. That point was settled" (221).

Gradually, Jane accepts the role she has chosen as the socially prominent wife of a highly respected, wealthy, conservative banker. She has an appropriately large suburban house with sufficient staff to run it perfectly. She has three children: Cicily, Jenny, and Steve. During the autumn, winter, and spring, she attends all the right social functions with all the right people. Every June, she and the children leave for the

Carver family summer estate on Boston's North Shore where
Stephen joins them for his three-week vacation in August.
However, after fifteen years of this ritualistic existence, Jane
feels that she has lost all sense of personal identity. She acts
her various roles as wife, mother, daughter, daughter-in-law,
and hostess according to the unalterable rules of social
convention, but she thinks: "In youth life seemed important.
The things you thought about *were* important, no matter how
inadequately you thought about them. But later you found
yourself involved in a labyrinth of trifles. Worrying, ridiculous
trifles. Things didn't matter, yet had to be coped with. And
you'd lost that sustaining sense, that any moment something
might be going to happen" (241).

IV *Years of Indecision*

The problem for Jane results from the social, familial pattern
of her life which irritates her. The dinner parties with the
same people saying the same things; the dull routine of
supervising household accounts; the tiresome meetings of
committees on which she serves because it is expected of her,
not because of any interest or sense of accomplishment she
derives from them. These stultifying trivialities make her wonder
"what life did to girls who were once young and full of
promise on Bryn Mawr window seats confidently assuming
that the world was their oyster . . ." (280).

Then Jimmy Trent, the wayward, clever husband of her
great friend Agnes, now a promising playwright, enters her
life. When he arrives in Chicago for the winter as a music
critic, his intellectuality challenges and awakens hers in a
fashion she had not experienced since she had left Bryn Mawr.
She loves to attend the concerts with him and to exchange
reactions with him about the performance; and, much to her
delight, she finds that he takes her ideas seriously. Her family
and friends surprise her by hailing him as a delightful social
addition, so they see each other under a wide variety of
circumstances. However, most meaningful to Jane is the realization that her interest and her encouragement have inspired
Jimmy to complete his violin concerto. What she refuses to
admit is that she has fallen in love with him.

Before Jimmy leaves for New York, he forces her to acknowledge the terrible reality of their love. The force of physical passion overwhelms her for the first time in her life; and, having no defense against her emotions, she agrees to elope with him. But, after a sleepless night of wrestling with her conscience, Jane knows she can neither leave Stephen nor permit herself to destroy Agnes' illusion of happiness; and she attempts to explain her reactions to Jimmy:

"This isn't just the silly reaction of a foolish woman to a moment's indiscretion. It's something much more serious. I'm in love with you, Jimmy, but I love you, too. I love you, just as I love Stephen and the children. I love you as I love Agnes. And that's one of the reasons why I won't let you do this thing. Can't I make you understand . . . what I mean? When you love people, you've got to be decent. You *want* to be decent. You want to be good. Just plain good—the way you were taught to be when you were a little child. Love is the greatest safeguard in the world against evil."

"Jane," he said, "Jane—you almost shake me . . . but it's silly—it's sentimental. It doesn't do anybody any good for a man and woman who are in love with each other to go on sordidly living with people they don't love. . . . I don't understand you. With all your innocence, you've always seemed so emancipated. Intellectually emancipated. You've always seemed to understand the complications of living."

"Oh, yes," said Jane, "I've done a lot of talking. . . . I was very smug about my tolerance. . . . I did believe it theoretically, Jimmy. But now—now when it comes to practice—I see there's a great difference."

"But there *isn't* any difference, Jane," said Jimmy. "Not any essential difference. Just one of convention . . . 'The Colonel's lady and Judy O'Grady are sisters under their skins!' "

"But they're *not*, Jimmy! That's just Kipling's revolt against Victorian prudery. . . . If you're really the Colonel's lady, Jimmy, no matter how little you want to do it, you know exactly what you ought to do." (364–66)

Jane cannot make Jimmy understand that fear of social ostracism and of economic uncertainty has no bearing upon her stand: that her feeling of human responsibility, which she cannot brush aside, has no place in his hedonistic code. Jimmy dies physically for Jane long before she learns of his

death as a German volunteer at the battle of the Marne.
However, the stimulus of Jimmy endures because, through their
relationship, she crystallizes her search for values begun years
before on the Bryn Mawr campus.

The feminism of M. Carey Thomas had stirred Jane intellectually to desire to explore the position of the woman outside
of the narrow confines set by social convention. However, she
had let that search go by default upon her marriage to Stephen;
and, through the years, she had forced herself to conform to
the traditional role. Her love for Jimmy awakens her keen but
dormant mind by challenging her accepted pattern of existence.
She emerges from this crisis with renewed inner strength
founded upon the firm belief in principle as the vital factor in
the determination of human behavior. In a very special sense,
she becomes a crusader. Although she never champions causes,
she does crusade by personal example for the maintenance of
human values which she sees threatened by the impact of
World War I.

V *Years of Decision*

The menace of the war becomes very real to Jane when
Cicily, lovely but willful at eighteen, demands to marry Jack
Bridges her first cousin, in a double ceremony with his sister
Belle and Albert Lancaster, Muriel's son, before the boys sail
for France. Jane recognizes the precarious foundation of this
marriage which has grown out of the unstable emotionalism
of wartime. Furthermore, she feels Cicily's restless temperament requires broader experiences before she settles upon
matrimony in the small circle in which she has grown up. In
Jane's futile efforts to persuade her daughter to choose college
instead of marriage, Jane grows alarmed about their totally
divergent viewpoint of freedom: "Lock herself up on a campus.
. . . That was what college life meant to the rising generation.
For her Bryn Mawr had spelled emancipation. Through Pembroke arch she had achieved a world of unprecedented freedom. Under the Bryn Mawr maples she had escaped from
family surveillance . . . from ideas with which she could never
agree, from standards to which she could never conform. . . .
To Cicily it seemed ridiculous servitude" (350).

Jane's apprehension about the future of Cicily and Jack increases in the aftermath of the war. At first, the birth of the twins Jane and John, followed by that of baby Robin, absorbs them; but a fierce argument arises over Jack's desire to do graduate work at Massachusetts Institute of Technology. Cicily balks because she hates Boston and the whole idea of being a student's wife; therefore she demands that Jack accept a position in Stephen's bank so they can build the French provincial house she has aways wanted and live in suburban Chicago among the family and friends whom they have known always. This stubborn inflexibility worries Jane. She deplores her daughter's intransigence in stifling Jack's ambition. Moreover, she also understands only too well that an immature, volatile young woman like Cicily might ultimately discover life in suburbia unendurable.

Although Cicily runs roughshod over Jack's hopes, she finds no satisfaction either in her house or in her mode of living. As she explains to Jane,

Do you know what I mean, Mumsy? Nothing ever happens to me. I sometimes feel as if these walls were just waiting to see something happen. Something *ought* to happen in a room as charming as this. I feel just that way about everything—Mumsy—about my clothes and the way I look and all the trouble about the maids and the meals and the children. I'm everlastingly setting the stage, but the drama never transpires. I'd like a little bit of drama. . . . Something nice and unexpected and exciting. Something different. Before I'm too old to enjoy it. . . . I've been married for nine years. I may be married for forty more. Am I just going to keep house . . . for forty years. Keep house and play bridge and go in town for dinner and have people out for Sunday luncheon—the same people. . . . I signed on the dotted line before I was old enough to know what I was doing. I don't mean that I really regret it. . . . Jack's always been sweet to me and I love my children. . . . Oh, I don't know what I want! Just girlhood over again, I guess. Just something else than this little front yard with the road to the station going by beyond the privet hedge, and Jack coming home from the five-thirty with a quart of gin in his pocket for a dinner-party full of people I couldn't care if I never saw again. (469–72)

Though Jane comprehends her daughter's frustration only too well, she questions Cicily's ability to work out a positive, lasting

solution. The war, she acknowledges, has unsettled the lives of
Cicily's generation and forced upon them problems with which
they lacked the maturity to cope. However, she believes that
Cicily and her contemporaries prefer to ignore the issues that
confront them and try in a hectic fashion to drive them away
through the pursuit of blind, idle pleasure.

The return of Belle and Albert and their three daughters from
Europe intensifies Cicily's discontentment. After his military
discharge, Albert had gone to Oxford to study international
relations in preparation for a foreign-service career. Very handsome and suave, he had matured and broadened into an
empathetic, perceptive young man. The combination of finances
and Belle's desire to lead a more settled existence causes him
to accept unwillingly a job in a Chicago aircraft plant.

A strong attraction rapidly develops between Cicily and
Albert. Physical appeal certainly accounts for part of it; but
more significant is their mutual feeling of thwarted adventure
and their keen desire to experience other ways of life that
leads them to fall in love. Despite family pleas, they are
determined upon divorce. In a final, agonizing interview Jane
begs Cicily to consider the havoc she is creating. Cicily retorts
calmly, "I'm not making havoc, any more than a surgeon who
performs a necessary operation. No one likes operations. They're
very unpleasant. But they save lives. People cry and carry on,
but later they're glad they had them. It takes time, of course,
to get over a major incision. But you wait. . . . In two years
time, we'll all be a great deal happier. A great deal happier
than we've been for years" (527).

Cicily's cool appraisal astounds her mother, and she finds it
virtually impossible to muster any reasonable argument against
its clear-sighted realism. As a last, desperate measure to deter
her, Jane tells Cicily about her renunciation of Jimmy. Her
daughter replies:

"I should think an experience like that would make you see how
wise I am to take my happiness."

"You don't achieve happiness," said Jane very seriously, "by
taking it."

"How do you know?" said Cicily promptly. "You never tried."

"I've always been happy," said Jane with dignity, "with your
father."

"I can't believe that . . . not after what you've told me."

"Well, I'm happy now," said Jane. "Much happier now than if—"

"But that's what you don't know, Mumsy!" cried Cicily smiling. "And what I'll never know either. You have to choose in life." (528–30)

This conversation with Cicily leaves Jane baffled. She cannot condone her course; yet neither can she condemn it. "But these children," she concedes readily, "had character. They had managed this appalling affair with extraordinary ability and restraint. They had a code . . . that was based on what? Bravado and barbarism or courage and common sense?" (534).

The only conclusion she reaches is that the members of this younger generation have bred out of their lives that very special but almost indefinable quality which for the want of a more specific word she calls "grace." However, despite that loss, Jane cannot deny that in time they may achieve a more vital and a more realistic approach to the solution of human problems. The subsequent revolts of her other children, Jenny and Steve, convince her that her children and their contemporaries have developed a positive assurance about their future which impresses Jane tremendously, even if it does not win her wholehearted approval.

Since her graduation from Bryn Mawr five years earlier, Jane's daughter Jenny and her roommate Barbara Belmont have longed to divide their time between running a kennel in Westchester County and taking a New York apartment for the winter season. Jenny announces firmly: "We're not marrying women—at least we never have been—we're interested in *ourselves*. We don't want to marry until we meet a man we fancy! In the meantime, we want to be independent. . . . I'm going to mess around in dirty tweeds in that heavenly country for eight months of the year and live very smartly in New York for the other four. I'm going to *enjoy* myself as I haven't since I left the Bryn Mawr campus" (519–20).

When Stephen recoils at his daughter's plan, Jenny insists that she is merely following in his footsteps, for he had chosen to live in Chicago instead of Boston. When he answers that the insurmountable difference is that she is a girl, Jane realizes that no one nurtured by the legacy of M. Carey Thomas will bow to that reasoning. While Jane admits she finds a toughness in Jenny's determination not usually equated with genteel femininity, she admires her strength of character which overrides every parental objection.

The revolt of Jane's son Steve is cleverly juxtaposed against that of his sisters'. His years at Milton Academy and at Harvard have converted him from a Chicagoan into a staunch New Englander. After his graduation from college, he returns to his father's bank because of a sense of filial obligation. He, following his sisters' example of striking for independence, proclaims he intends to move into a little, red-brick colonial house on Beacon Hill, furnish it with the best antiques, and reign as Boston's most courted bachelor. He concludes with a flourish: "On my twenty-ninth birthday, I'm going to marry the season's most eligible debutante—and her name will be Cabot or Lodge or Lowell—and replenish the dwindling Carver stock. I'm going to have children in the good old New England tradition, and marry them off to the best Back Bay connections. There! That's a brief résumé of my earthly plans and ambitions" (515–16).

The decisions of the younger Carvers provide a nice touch of irony. To a generation and to a class that view an advantageous marriage and motherhood as the prize goals for ladies the respective courses deliberately chosen by Cicily and Jenny seem to be sheer self-destruction. However, that same generation and class also made something of a fetish of the importance of the pioneer spirit in the male. Thus, while there can be no question of Steve's choice being socially unacceptable, nonetheless it is dismaying. Somehow he appears to have renounced his masculine sense of independence.

Steve's decision particularly confounds his mother, for she cannot comprehend how anyone can embrace so enthusiastically the intransigent traditionalism of Beacon Hill nor does she understand how he can choose so freely to live in the past and to relinquish the adventure of the present. Nevertheless, she appreciates the self-assurance that enables Steve, like his sisters, to know so absolutely what he desires to do with his life.

Only Cicily's future really upsets Jane. As her Paris divorce becomes final, her parents admit that, while they deplore her move, they want to be with her on her wedding day. Moreover, the trip to France means to Jane an opportunity for a reunion with André, now renowned as a sculptor and a favorite with international society. However much she may disapprove of divorce, Jane has to agree that she has never seen Cicily so radiantly happy and that Albert, in addition to charm and good looks, does possess an intelligence and a seriousness of purpose that relieve some of her anxiety about their marriage. On the other hand, she finds the meeting with André profoundly disturbing.

Upon her visit to André's studio, Jane is shocked by what she considers to be a great deterioration in both the man and the sculptor. She acknowledges his most recent work is graceful and lovely, but it utterly lacks the strength of his earlier pieces. Like his art, she discovers that André has grown into a cynical esthete. When he asks her what great emotional experience she has known in the years since they parted, she replies that her marriage to Stephen has been the most important thing that has happened to her. André appears incredulous; then he asserts that it makes no difference because all experiences end in blind alleys. She fears her vehement refutation makes her seem ridiculously priggish. Returning to her hotel, Jane reviews her life:

If she had had Cicily's conviction . . . she might have married André and remarried Stephen and run away with Jimmy. Her life might have been more interesting for those forbidden experiments. But she would not have been the same Jane at fifty-one. Not that Jane thought so much of the Jane she was. Or did she? Did you not always think a little too tenderly of the kind of person that you turned out to be?

Cicily had been right about one thing. You had to choose in life. And perhaps you never gave up anything except what some secret self-knowledge whispered you did not really care to possess. But no . . . she had made her sacrifices in agony of spirit. She had made them in simplicity and sincerity. . . . But to what end?

For Cicily had been right about another thing. You did not know —you could not ever tell—just where the path you had not taken would have led you.

To what end, then, did you struggle to live with dignity and decency and decorum. . . . Was it only to cultivate in your own character that intangible quality . . . grace? Was it only to feel self-respectful on your deathbed? That seemed a barren reward. (576–78)

Jane cannot accept the premise that, if she had acted upon any hedonistic principle, she would have had a happier life. Nevertheless, she admits that she can judge only from rather limited experience. She has conformed, at least outwardly, to the thoroughly conventional standards in which she was brought up. But, more than just conforming to them, she realizes she attaches real value to the dignity and orderliness in life those standards impose.

However, she knows also that there exists that other side of her personality that questions the validity of the conventional attitudes. She is aware that she has never been able to submerge that shadowy self that responds to the ideals of M. Carey Thomas and Bryn Mawr, that never allows her to lose faith in the educated woman, that forces her to the reluctant feeling that she somehow cannot accept the traditional feminine role. While she is sometimes torn between two opposed viewpoints toward life, she never falls prey to frustration. She discovers too much stimulus in the process of living with its challenging alternatives of choice and its fascinating interplay of human relationships to be ensnared by self-pity. At fifty-one, she can review the past with candor but without rancor.

Yet, although she shares much of the younger generation's faith in the future, she cannot completely dismiss the idea that her children do not seem to be doing "more" with their lives than she and her contemporaries have done. Steve desires Beacon Hill in order to preserve the past. Cicily, for all her sharing Albert's love of the foreign-service, relishes any kind of existence that offers the romance and adventure of travel and new places. Jenny, who loved every aspect of college life, asks for nothing more than to preside over a smart New York salon. It is not that Jane herself has ever aspired to do something "worthwhile"; nor does she care especially that none of her children show any inclination to lead "causes." Nevertheless, she cannot escape the thought that there is something missing in a society that manages to stifle those glowing hopes for the future that she had heard discussed so avidly on Bryn Mawr window seats.

There is certainly nothing exceptionally original about either the theme or the characters of *Years of Grace*. Although many

authors have covered much of the same ground, not too many
of them have traversed it with such distinction. Urbanity, wit,
and total objectivity distinguish this work at every turn. And
perhaps not the least of the author's accomplishments is that
she holds the reader's interest to the very last page.

One critic considered that the novel reflected the Realistic
strength that made the fiction of Theodore Dreiser so remarkable.[2] Probably it would be more accurate to say that
Mrs. Barnes's work is closer to that of William Dean Howells
than to that of Dreiser; but she definitely belongs to the Realist
tradition. She placed great emphasis upon the importance of
historical accuracy even in minor detail in the writing of the
novel.[3] To enhance the historicity she included real figures.
Thus she made Marion Park, the dean of Radcliffe and
president of Bryn Mawr, a college classmate and great friend
of Jane Carver. Margaret Barnes also believed that the funda-
mental purpose of the American novelist should be to record
the voices and moods of America.[4] Her approach to literature
resembled very much that of the primitive to painting.

She displayed, like all the other Realists, a wonderful eye
for detail, as well as an excellent ability to use minutiae, to
convey the atmosphere of different eras and generations. We
have, for example, the description of the Carvers' Beacon Hill
house:

The furniture in the Carvers' front parlour was oddly assorted.
The Colonial period rubbed elbows with the Victorian age. There
were several good eighteenth century pieces that had been in the
family for generations and, mingled with them, were the rosewood
"parlour suite" that Mrs. Carver had bought in the first year of
her marriage, and a triple-tiered black-walnut whatnot that had
been left to Mr. Carver in the will of a favourite sister, and an old
cerise plush armchair, with a fringe of braided tassels . . . and a
large glass cabinet of Chinese Chippendale design in which were
displayed a collection of curios assembled by long-dead Carvers in
the course of their voyages on the whale-ships and merchantmen
that had carried them over the seven seas—ivory piecutters and
paperknives and bodkins, a set of Chinese beads . . . a tiny model
of a clipper ship, miraculously erect in a small-necked rum bottle,
tortoise-shell snuff-boxes, ebony chessmen, sandalwood fans, a bronze
Javanese gong of intricate pattern, and a small marble replica of

the Leaning Tower of Pisa. Also a first edition of Oliver Wendell Holmes's "The School Boy," personally autographed and inscribed to Mr. Carver by Mr. Holmes. (507)

In contrast to the description of the elder Carvers' living room, Mrs. Barnes depicts Jenny Carver's New York penthouse in the 1920's and her parents' reaction to it: "The penthouse was small and very, very modern. Jane could not understand its scheme of decoration. From the Euclid designs of the geometric silver furniture to the tank of living goldfish set in the marble walls of Jenny's black bathroom, it all looked very queer to Jane. It looked queerer to Stephen. His face had been a study when he had seen the goldfish" (542).

Because of the same attention to small detail, Margaret Barnes managed to reproduce graphic thumbnail sketches of minor characters. She did so in a particularly telling fashion in her portrayal of Jane's initial impression of her Carver in-laws when she meets them at the railroad station upon their arrival in Chicago for the wedding:

There were six of them and all very friendly, indeed. Except for their short, clipped accent and a certain funny something that they did, or rather did not do, to their r's, they might have been born and bred on Pine Street. Stephen's mother . . . was short and plump, with . . . pale, protruding eyes and iron grey hair . . . she had very little to say. This deficiency was more than made up for by the fact that Stephen's father had a great deal to say. Mr. Alden Carver was a very impressive gentleman. He was grey-haired, too, and he had a close-clipped grey Vandyke beard and moustache, and shrewd light-blue eyes that peered out from under his grey eyebrows with an uncanny resemblance to Stephen's. His cheeks looked very soft and pink above the close-clipped grey beard. His collars and cuffs were very white and glossy and his grey sack suit was in perfect press.

Alden Carver, Junior . . . told Jane, immediately, on the platform of the train shed, with all the air of placing himself for her, once and for all, that he was in the Class of '88, at Harvard.

Stephen's sister Silly [Cicily] . . . was thirty-one. . . . Jane had thought she was perfectly stunning when she saw her get off the train in her blue serge suit and crisp white shirt waist and small black sailor. A perfect Gibson girl. Slim and distinguished. But that night at dinner . . . she had not looked nearly as well in evening dress. Somehow lank and mannish, in spite of blue taffeta, long-limbed and angular, and, yes, distinctly old. She didn't seem like a sister at all to Stephen. More like an aunt.

Stephen had an aunt, who had come too, with his uncle who was his father's brother. The Stephen Carver for whom Stephen had been named. . . . He was a college professor in Cambridge . . . and his field was Restoration Drama. Jane knew all about Restoration Drama and she knew all about college professors. It made her remember Bryn Mawr very vividly, just to see his wrinkled brown tweed suit and gold-bowed spectacles. His dinner coat was just a little shiny.

Uncle Stephen's wife was Aunt Marie. She looked like the wives of all college professors, thought Jane. Nice and bright and friendly and not too careful about how she did her hair. (211–12)

As many reviewers noted, *Years of Grace* must be judged as a study in social history, as well as a work of fiction.[5] It would not be going too far to say that the novel is as much a portrait of an era as it is the fictional biography of Jane Ward Carver.

A particularly interesting aspect of Mrs. Barnes's interpretation of her period was her view of the decade of the 1890's as the "watershed" of American social history, to use the image of Professor Henry Steele Commager.[6] Once again she employed the minute to demonstrate the shifting social codes and mores; and the view of Jane reflects the force of change; she challenges, for example, the relevance of the accepted standards from her refusal to agree with the family edict that she must not work on an English translation of Dumas' *La Dame aux Camélias* (because Sarah Bernhardt is an immoral woman and thus the play is immoral) to her spirited defense of Lily Furness' suicide.

Lily Furness, the lovely, fascinating mother of Jane's great friend Flora, is a memorable minor character. For many years she has been having an affair with Bert Lancaster, a dashing man-about-town who, in age, is halfway between Lily and her debutante daughter Flora. Society has watched with envy the course of the affair because, to all outward appearance, their behavior is impeccable; and the youthful beauty, genuine sweetness, and audacity of Lily are envied quietly by many matrons. Lily faces the future with complete realism: she knows that her beauty will fade and that Lancaster will ultimately marry one of the most eligible debutantes. If her passion for him is the center of her existence, she understands that a combination of vanity and notoriety prompts him to continue the liaison. At the end of Flora's and Jane's debut year, he becomes engaged to their friend Murial Lester, who is strikingly handsome, wealthy, and very high spirited; and both Flora and Jane are bridesmaids. In the packed church, every eye is cocked to see whether Lily Furness will appear; however, when Flora and her father had left for the church, Lily had committed suicide.

This act outrages proper society. Jane's mother, Mrs. Ward, and Stephen Carver, Lily's nephew, view the suicide as a disgrace and as "common" because it transgresses Christian ethics and social convention, respectively. Jane knows about the affair since being a debutante means that she can learn the social, if not the physical, facts of life. She refutes the opinions of her mother and Stephen:

Jane suddenly realized that Stephen Carver had seen her tears. He was looking down at her very tenderly . . .
"Jane—don't!" said Stephen. . . . He looked very understanding.
"It's just that Mamma—" faltered Jane. "Mamma shouldn't talk so."
"It *is* a disgrace," said Stephen solemnly.
Jane felt terribly shocked. He didn't understand at all, after all.
"Oh—no!" she said faintly. "It's just—tragedy." Stephen still stared at her, quite uncomprehending. "Never—disgrace," said Jane. "She loved him."
Stephen was looking at her as if he found her words quite unintelligible. Jane slipped through the front door. Her mother, on the front steps, was still talking volubly to Mrs. Lester. . . .
Jane silently followed them down to the sidewalk. She felt strangely calm and exalted. A finished life was a very solemn, a very splendid thing. She didn't care what her mother said, now. Death had an unassailable dignity.
"And it's not only a disgrace," her mother was murmuring earnestly. "The whole thing seems so terribly sordid—turning on the gas like that—in a bathroom—like any woman of the streets. Lily Furness had always so much pride."
" 'I have lived and accomplished the task that Destiny gave me,' " thought Jane very solemnly [recalling her favorite lines from Vergil on the death of Dido], " 'and now I shall pass beneath the earth no common shade.' " (165–66)

With *Years of Grace* Margaret Ayer Barnes produced "a substantial and satisfying piece of work, substantial in the large and immediate sense of life it conveys, and satisfying in the sureness of its procedure, the rightness of its effect. . . ."[7] In addition, she wrote a very fine panorama of an era; for she infused her chronicle with "the tones of life itself, . . . enlivening them at every turn with some gesture or inflection expressing witty criticism or shrewd courageous comment."[8]

CHAPTER 4

Westward Passage

W ESTWARD PASSAGE (1931), Margaret Barnes's second novel, depicts the transatlantic crossing of Olivia Van Tyne Ottendorf, who with her young daughter Olivia, is returning to Chicago from a Paris shopping expedition as the first step in the preparations for young Olivia's debut season. Olivia discovers among the other passengers Nicholas Allen, her former husband, the father of young Olivia, and a distinguished author. During the course of the voyage, they decide they have fallen in love again; as a result, they escape to his Vermont farm where they had spent their first honeymoon. However, they find nothing has changed: they are still impossible for each other.

At first glance, *Westward Passage* might seem to fit into the category of the typical "society" novel that used to appear so often in serial form in the popular magazines; but such is not the case. Although the novel moves swiftly and reads easily, Mrs. Barnes wrote with a more serious purpose than mere entertainment. She was concerned with presenting a study of one particular type of woman produced by the social tradition of the upper middle class, and her shrewd characterization of Olivia gives substance to the work as a whole.

I *Before the Crossing*

The characterization of Olivia Ottendorf makes a nice contrast to that of Jane Carver in *Years of Grace*. Both women find it difficult to adhere to the conventional society to which they belong. Indeed, both of them succeed momentarily in breaking out of that constrained circle: Jane, through Bryn Mawr, Olivia, through her first marriage to the bohemian

Nick Allen. These vital, youthful influences prove to be the decisive factors in shaping their personalities. Jane develops a strong sense of realism derived from her reflections on people and events, but Olivia harbors the false illusion of herself as an inspiration to artists. At fifty-one Jane has come to grips with herself and her limitations; on the other hand, Olivia at thirty-nine cannot bear the thought that in another year she will be remembered only as the mother of a debutante.

Olivia's problem springs from no resentment at the popularity of her daughter but from the fear that she herself cannot survive without masculine adulation. She cannot distract her thoughts from the overwhelming dread of the winter in Chicago that lies ahead of her, for the only thing about that season that will distinguish it from the other ten she has known as the wife of Harry Ottendorf is that she will have to accept somehow being cast in the role of young Olivia's mother: first, as mother of the debutante; then, as mother of the bride; and, finally, as a grandmother.

Olivia wants male admirers, not lovers:

There was nothing like a man and his flattery, she reflected with a pensive sigh, to make a woman remember that life is not over at whatever age she happened to be. Not that she had ever gone in for philandering. Why hadn't she?—When her life with Nick had proved so unhappy and her life with Harry was proving so dull and she had come so increasingly to feel that she had never really lived and never really *would* live before she died. Olivia would be forty on her next birthday. She shivered when she thought of it. You couldn't laugh off forty. Forty was middle-aged.[1]

Despite her vanity and her egocentricity, Olivia harbors no illusions about herself. She never attempts to excuse herself for the unhappiness of her first marriage and for the boredom of her second; her failure, she recognizes, results from weakness, not hardness. She understands that she refuses to contend with the routine in marriage because she must exist always in the aura of romance. Furthermore, she realizes her exaggerated romantic need grew out of the cold practicality that had been imposed upon her by her parents, who, impecunious scions of two of New York's most aristocratic families, had dared to marry for love. In their straitened circumstances, the

Van Tynes had made it blatantly clear that they expected their three daughters to recoup the family fortune through advantageous marriages.

When Olivia, the loveliest, had eloped with Nick Allen, an unemployed would-be author, her father "had felt exactly as if a trusted bank had failed him" (8). Her sister Ruth had somewhat redeemed Olivia's disgrace by capturing Hendriks Bleecker with his lavish estate at Oyster Bay. The parental elation had soared when Diana had chosen Prince Guido Arezzo and had taken her place as a lady-in-waiting to the Queen of Italy. Ultimately, Olivia had incurred family favor by divorcing Nick after ten years of discontentment and by marrying Harry Ottendorf, the heir of a Milwaukee brewer who had made his own fortune in a Chicago brokerage. At her second wedding, her father "had had the incredible feeling that an investment which had long ceased to pay dividends had suddenly sent him a check for his accrued losses" (*Ibid.*).

Olivia has never forgotten her first meeting with Harry Ottendorf at an ultraconventional Park Avenue dinner party, the kind of function which Nick had particularly loathed and which he had attended simply because his wife had insisted upon it. Harry's flattering attention made her oblivious to her unfashionable evening dress and her scratched silver slippers. At the end of the evening, when he had invited her to lunch the next day, she had accepted with unusual excitement. The following morning, when a corsage of eight orchids arrived, she had felt amused and intrigued:

Laughing a little, Olivia had pinned them on the coat of her threadbare blue suit and had glanced at herself in the mirror and had thought that their florid exuberance made her look a trifle common. . . . She could see the reflection that had laughed back at her from the mirror—pretty and shabby and only twenty-nine— and she could remember the thrill of excitement with which she had reflected that, though the brilliant orchids on the threadbare suit made her look like an erring stenographer, they also made her look young and gay and popular again, and her reckless sensation of worldly sophistication when she resolved to forget, for an hour or two, that she was Nicholas Allen's indigent young wife and that she ought to stay at home and eat hamburger steak with her eight-year-old daughter, and had opened the door of her Greenwich Village flat and had gone to meet Harry for luncheon at Pierre's. (2–3)

During the luncheon at Pierre's, Olivia had found Harry marvelously different from Nick. After ten years of trying to cope unsuccessfully with Nick's mercurial brilliance, Harry's pedestrian qualities had held a peculiar fascination for her. She had fallen in love with Harry, not his money; and, after meeting him, her relationship with Nick had rapidly deteriorated. She had agreed that the confining atmosphere of the tiny Greenwich Village flat with an active child was very difficult for a writer; but the attempt to keep house on a very limited budget was excruciating for her. Although Nick had managed to scrape together enough money to send little Olivia to a private school and to provide a maid, neither of them had known any economic security or much physical happiness during their married years. And so they had parted: Olivia, to marry Harry; Nick, to win acclaim as an author. They have not met until they find themselves on the same luxury liner on a voyage across the Atlantic.

II *In Mid-Ocean*

Seeing Nick sweeps away the years for Olivia, for he symbolizes not only her youthful allure but also the panacea for her adjustment to the forthcoming winter:

If she could have those five brief days alone with Nick—to laugh and talk and—yes—be just a trifle divinely, but harmlessly silly with him. Those five brief days alone with Nick . . . would quite set her up for the winter that would follow them. They would make her realize that, though she was almost forty and little Olivia was "coming out," there was still something attractive and amusing and young about her! They would delude her into thinking for a moment that life was not over at thirty-nine. (61-62)

If Olivia longs only for a harmless shipboard flirtation, Nick professes ardently that he has never ceased to love her. She slips easily into the atmosphere of romance on which she thrives, but she recognizes also that she must subtly impress upon him that she is very much Harry's faithful wife. Finally, she concludes that she must not see him again except as his hostess if he should visit Chicago; and she imagines that occasion:

In her own drawing-room, swept and garnished as it was by the hand of the modern decorator, denuded of every homely object that had reference to their mutual past, she would feel mistress of herself and of the situation. Behind her own tea-tray, pouring her China tea out of the silver teapot that was part of the Georgian service which Harry had bought for her in London on their wedding trip, she would feel as serene and unruffled as the vast plane of pale-blue water that stretched before her fifteenth story windows. She would feel like what she was. She would feel like Harry's wife.

Nick, too, sitting on her jade-green sofa with his feet on her pale grey rug, noting the oyster-white walls and the silver hanging and the sparsely scattered, perfectly-placed chairs and tables—collector's pieces, everyone!—breathing the faint clean perfume from the great bowl of white roses which stood beside her tea-table, looking from his self-possessed hostess to her self-possessed reflection in the crystal mirror above the black mantelpiece. . . . Nick would face that fact that bygones *were* bygones.

She was Olivia Ottendorf—Mrs. Harry Ottendorf—irrevocably transmuted by the alchemy of time and experience from the soft, silly, wistful, idealistic young creature who had run off with him—from "the kid that had married him"—into—well, into something quite different, at any rate, from the girl she had been, or the woman she might have become, if she had remained Olivia Allen—Mrs. Nicholas Allen in the Greenwich Village flat. (154–55)

However, all of Olivia's intentions melt before Nick's ardor; she knows he is the love of her life. Her destiny, she decides with romantic flourish, lies in sparking his artistic genius. But, when she seeks and hears Olivia's opinion of her father, her daughter's attitude shocks her into a recognition of what Nick and Harry are in themselves. Little Olivia explains:

It seemed to me . . . that no matter *what* he'd done, he'd come out at the small end of the horn. We were all happy. But he—well. I used to think of him. There's some appeal about the underdog to me. The one who got left. . . . Now that I've seen him, I don't see how you could have lived with him ten days, let alone ten years. . . . What I wish you'd tell me now . . . is why you ever fell for him? He's such a queer mixture—so cocksure one minute and so sentimental the next. I think he's awfully conceited—in a rather subtle way. He's very light and airy about himself, of course, and he's funny—but he always knows he's funny. He likes to be laughed at and applauded and admired. He likes to make a hit with the

ladies. I suppose what he really likes is just to be loved—which is
rather pathetic. For how *could* you love anything quite so bright and
glittering and shiny.... You're worth ten of him. (162–63)

This candid appraisal of Nick reminds Olivia sharply of
the vast differences between her two husbands. Furthermore,
it jolts her into the uncomfortable awareness that perhaps the
glamorous vision of herself as a celebrity's wife has warped
her moral sense. She realizes how much she owes to Harry
and sees any thought of romance with Nick as unworthy and
clandestine: everything she cannot tolerate. When she tells
Nick they must give up each other, he bursts out passionately:

"Livvy, darling... have you thought what's ours for the taking.
... What does life hold as you're living it now?"
"It holds a great deal, Nick, that you have no conception of."
"Material things? I could make you very comfortable, Livvy. I—"
"Not that... not that at all. You *do* think me mercenary, Nick,
don't you?"
"No... But you might well consider—"
"I'm not considering anything... but personal relationships... you
—you don't seem to visualize Harry's position."
"Harry's position? I visualized my own, ten years ago. Harry's
only getting what's coming to him. It's poetic justice—"
"No... it's *not* poetic justice. I can't explain, Nick, but Harry's
not at all like you. He—he *deserves* to be happy."
"Well, good God! Didn't I deserve to be happy?"
"Not—not quite in the same sense that Harry does.... You see,
Nick,—he—he's quite an unusual person. You were unusual, too, of
course. You've proved that. But Harry's unusual in quite a different
way. He's proved it, too. In ten long years of marriage, Harry's
never had a thought for himself. He's been kind and gentle and
generous. He's been—child-like. He—"
"He hasn't made you happy... in spite of all his virtues."
"I sometimes think, Nick... that must have been my fault...
I ought to be happy with Harry."
"But you're not... it doesn't make much difference where the
fault lies." (183–86)

Olivia leaves the ship without seeing Nick again; but that
evening she receives a telegram from him at her parents' house,
informing her that he will wait for her at midnight at the

gate to Gramercy Park. The message shatters her resolve, for
it evokes the enchantment of being nineteen and of meeting
Nick in the same secret tryst as she had twenty years ago.

III *The End of the Voyage*

In the park flooded by moonlight, Nick's proposal of elopement intoxicates Olivia; it gives her the opportunity to relive
her life with the advantage of maturity. Nevertheless, she
cannot overcome completely the apprehensive thought that,
should the outcome of this second romance with Nick be the
same, there will be no Harry waiting in the wings. The seductive atmosphere batters down her every defense; she consents
to go with him to the Vermont farm. Having made her decision,
Olivia steals back to her bedroom in a state of ecstasy just
as she had done at nineteen. However, her rapturous mood
vanishes with the realization that she must write to Harry.
Try as she will, she cannot think of any explanation to give
him. She knows that she has made no effort to air her feelings
of discontentment and that she has allowed invisible barriers
to separate them without his being aware that they existed.
Her excuse becomes her vague belief that she and Nick will
create that paradise of which she has dreamed for twenty
years, but she leaves to meet Nick with the letter still unwritten.

Motoring to Vermont with Nick, Olivia drifts blissfully into
a reverie about her future in which she envisions herself as a
literary hostess presiding over an artistic colony whose members will make really significant contributions to the world.
In her mind's eye she works out elaborate plans of how she
will renovate the old farmhouse so that it will retain its austere
New England charm while being transformed into a handsome
estate suitable for a celebrated author and his socialite wife.

After an idyllic, harmonious trip through the beautiful New
England autumn, they settle before a roaring open fire in the
living room for cocktails. Olivia confides excitedly all the mar-
velous ideas she has formulated for redoing the house. A look
of horror passes over Nick's face as he listens. He replies tersely:

"No, Livvy, we can't live on that scale."
"But, Nick," said Olivia earnestly, "we *have* to live on it."
"Why?"

"Because people do—because everyone does."

"No one in Greenfield does."

"Oh, Nick!" cried Olivia in exasperation. "We know how people live who live in other places. It isn't as if we didn't have the money, Nick. You've been extremely successful and you've never spent a cent. If you *didn't* have it, I'd be the first to say we ought to economize. But as it is, I think it's time you took your place in the community. You ought to make your home attractive and ask attractive people to come to it. It's just *lazy* of you to settle down and go native."

"Livvy," he said presently, "you must get this. It isn't just the money. . . . But even if I had millions, I couldn't stand the racket. Attractive people don't attract me when I'm trying to write. Writing's my life, Livvy—you must remember that. All I want in the world is a little peace and a desk in a good light and three square meals a day and—"

"And me," said Olivia in a very small, low voice. "You said you wanted me."

"Of course, I want you. You know I do."

"Nick," she said solemnly, "you told me on the boat that you had faced the inconvenience of living with a woman."

"I thought I had! I'd forgotten how women like to *run* things. There's a practical, pushing side to a woman, Livvy, that's enough to appall any man. It appalls me—I tell you frankly. Here you haven't been two hours in this farmhouse and you're already talking about pulling it down and building it up again—"

"Don't forget," said Olivia tartly, "that I've been here before."

"That's why I thought you knew what you were getting in for."

"I did know!" protested Olivia. "But I thought it would be different now you have—" Olivia stopped suddenly. She was striving for perfect honesty, but expressing it in words, perfect honesty seemed a trifle crude. She had not stopped in time, however.

"More money?" said Nick. "Livvy, that's all you think of."

"I don't!" cried Olivia. "It's you that thinks of money! I think of comfort and convenience."

"It's neither comfort nor convenience," remarked Nick acidly, "to live in a manner that you can't afford. You must remember, Livvy, that you've had ten years with a multimillionaire. . . . I wonder . . . if you've ever faced the inconvenience of living with a writer?"

"Faced it!" cried Olivia scornfully. "Didn't I live with you for ten years in the Greenwich Village flat!" (303–7)

Without another word, Nick leaves her and goes outside; but, as soon as he has closed the door, he realizes the catastrophe of his outburst. He returns to Olivia quickly, urging her to come out and look at the beauty of the starlit night which will make them forget their idiotic quarrel. Olivia follows silently, for their argument has sobered her. Their folly, as she sees with brutal clarity, lies in their naïveté in thinking they can recapture a past that had never existed.

Unlike Nick, Olivia faces herself. The idea of the adventure which life with Nick offers intrigues her from afar; but, when forced to choose, she knows she wants the security in every sense of that word which Harry provides. Nick, disbelieving what he sees happening, watches her get into the car. In desperation, he pleads with her to stay; but Olivia answers:

"I'd spoil everything. Everything you like best . . . I'm just the sort of person you can't bear to have around. . . . I'm waking up from a dream. For ten years, I've been cherishing the delusion that we wouldn't have quarrelled if we hadn't been young and foolish— that—that I still loved you, really. . . . Well—now we're middle-aged. . . . We really are, Nick, though we don't feel so. And yet we did it again. We'd always do it. We haven't changed a bit. . . . Write a great novel, Nick! I know you will!"

"Oh, Livvy! Shut *up*!" The absurd words in their anguished accents plucked suddenly at her heartstrings.

"I will. Oh, Nick, dear! Don't look like that! Don't—don't *feel* like that!"

As she spoke, Olivia leaned over the wheel. She kissed his upturned face. His hands stretched out to her.

"Livvy—you're crying!"

"Of course I'm crying!" sobbed Olivia hysterically. "Why wouldn't I cry?"

Before he could answer, she set the gears in motion. She pulled herself from his arms. The Chrysler moved slowly around the little turn-around. (309–14)

Driving to the nearby inn, Olivia panics at the thought of the telephone call she must make to Harry. The fear of his rejection terrifies her, but her own experience has taught her that no true happiness between them can exist unless she gives him the same freedom of choice that she has taken. Harry never falters; in his simple, direct fashion he tells her that he will take the night train to meet her in Boston.

IV *Critical Reactions*

One critic judged *Westward Passage*: "The women's magazines are full of stories of this type at the present. Margaret Ayer Barnes just happened to write what is probably the best of them."[2] Some justification exists for this assessment, particularly when this novel is compared to *Years of Grace*; for the initial impression is that *Westward Passage* seems contrived. However, a closer look refutes this first opinion because the perceptive characterizations and the astute comments of Margaret Barnes do provide substance to an otherwise shallow, flimsy plot.[3]

Mrs. Barnes explained her attitude about the technical challenges of this novel:

The thing that interested me most about writing "Westward Passage" after "Years of Grace" was the handling of the time element. ... The action of "Westward Passage" takes place in seven days. Yet the plot demands that the lives of the three principal characters Nick, Olivia, and the unseen Harry must be revealed to the reader in toto through the medium of speech or reflection. All the emotional changes that they have experienced during the last twenty years must be made clear by the end of the last chapter. ... The ocean liner serves as a hothouse in which the relationship between Nick and Olivia ripens with a rapidity that it never would in a more normal environment. All the action takes place "on the spot." The reader is asked to believe nothing whatever on the statement of the author. As in a play, certain things occur, certain things are said; the reader sees and hears them through the eyes and ears of Olivia and witnesses her resulting reactions.[4]

Although Mrs. Barnes admirably achieved her stated objectives, *Westward Passage* is only partially successful as a novel. From the viewpoint of technique, the work shows an adept use of "the classic device" of building suspense by offering series after series of alternatives, so plausible and counterbalanced, that the novel does challenge the reader to the final page.[5] Furthermore, Mrs. Barnes used the flashback very deftly, and an excellent example of this device is the introduction of the unseen Harry Ottendorf. The reader visualizes Harry through the thoughts of Olivia, who, while dining at the cap-

tain's table with her former husband Nick Allen, contrasts her
two husbands:

> She had had ten years of watching Harry's face across dinner-
> tables—Harry's round, amiably Teutonic face, with the blond hair
> growing just a little thick above the temples and the plump cheeks
> growing just a little heavy above the jaw. Ten years of watching
> Harry's round face grow blank as an empty plate, as Harry deliberately
> considered what he could think of to say next, while the woman
> on one side of him turned defiantly a naked indifferent shoulder
> and the woman on the other toyed pensively with the stem of her
> wineglass or nibbled a meditative olive in silence.
> God knew Olivia had always felt married to Harry on *those*
> occasions! She had felt acutely that absurd sense of responsibility—
> that ridiculous extension of the ego to the person and peculiarities
> of another human being—that was the essential character of the
> united married state. At her own parties, at such psychological
> moments Olivia had always thrown out the lifeline. (85–86)

In addition to the contrast of personalities and social capa-
bilities in this description of Harry's discomfiture, Margaret
Barnes made particularly fine use of detailed descriptions of
architecture, landscaping, and décor not only to point to
difference in social outlook but also to emphasize Olivia's
imagined reasons for her dissatisfaction with her marriage to
Harry as well as their difference in taste and their cultural
backgrounds:

> Olivia veritably believed that Harry, in spite of his ten years of resi-
> dence in her intensively interior-decorated Lake Shore Drive apartment,
> still stubbornly thought that the Ottendorf mansion [in Milwaukee]
> was beautiful! Still stubbornly admired its shiny white, terra-cotta-
> tiled walls, topped with its shiny green, terra-cotta-tiled roof which
> rose in spotless Teutonic splendour from its acres of close-clipped
> turf, geometrically bisected with gravel paths and dotted with
> circular flower-beds of red and yellow tulips in the spring and red
> and pink geraniums in the summer and fall. Olivia veritably believed
> that Harry even stubbornly admired the largest flower-bed of all,
> which adorned the turn-around in front of the house, in which the
> name of the Ottendorf mansion, "Friedenheim," was spelled out in
> nameless herbs, magenta, and page-green colour. Olivia veritably
> believed that Harry still stubbornly admired the gleaming silver

glass gazing-ball which stood on a shiny white, terra-cotta-tiled pedestal in the centre of the lawn, reflecting the turf and the paths and the flower-beds and the mansion in distorted miniature and the great iron fence, with its shiny white terra-cotta-tiled posts, each topped with its little green terra-cotta-tiled roof. And the glittering glass greenhouse. And the shiny white, terra-cotta-tiled garage. And the rococo German summer house on the bluff overlooking the lake where Mrs. Ottendorf served coffee and *Krauz-kuchen*, every pleasant spring, summer, and autumn afternoon to the most conventional German-American society in Milwaukee! (16–17)

As in all of her fiction, Mrs. Barnes created memorable minor figures. In *Westward Passage,* the shipboard setting provided her with an excellent opportunity to present her impressions of the distinctive features of the international upper middle class and aristocratic group, as in the following graphic portraits of an American and a British woman of the fashionable world:

Henrietta [Parsons of New York], looking incredibly smart and slim in a black-covert-cloth suit and a black skull cap, pushed fashionably back from her high, white forehead, outlining her delicate hatchet face with the felicity of line and contour of some early Florentine canvas. Henrietta . . . looked just as much like a cameo as she did like a hatchet, and even more like some long dead, high-born lady who had made the pulse of a Renaissance painter beat a little faster.
    Lady Coverly was standing beside her, bunched up in heather-coloured British-tweeds, a cane in her hand and a long mauve complexion veil, floating ridiculously from the tan grouse that was flattened against the crown of her heather-coloured tweed hat. English women were amazing. . . . Bunched up and ridiculous in those weather-beaten clothes, grey-haired and sixty, if a day, there was an air of pleasant, commanding authority about Lady Coverly, an atmosphere of genial, quite-taken-for-granted aristocracy, that made the finely etched distinction of Henrietta Parsons look brittle and spurious and shoddy—just a matter of dressmakers and complexion salons. (62–63)

Although these portraits add verve to the narrative, they are extraneous because they do very little to illuminate the relationship between Olivia and Nick.
    Equally notable was her ability to enliven her rather hum-

drum narrative with her characters' keen comments about men
or about human motives, as, for example, Nick's comment about
novelists:

"Good novelists are merely people who possess a sense of reality
and a gift for telling a story. They're people who are willing to work
like dogs and think only of themselves—for your book is yourself . . .
it's an extension of the ego. Artists are always egotistical and usually
mean. They're muckers, really—"

"Nick!" protested Olivia.

"But they are, Livvy! Just that impulse to give yourself away—
there's something muckerish about that—"

"It's only the impulse to tell the truth!" cried Olivia.

"It's the impulse to tell the world," muttered Nick moodily. "You
don't know, Livvy—that rotten urge of the writer in the most
passionate situations to stand off and observe—to record and remember—to take notes on your emotional reactions—on your very
words sometimes—for future reference. To sell yourself. Not for
gold, perhaps—but for glory." (172–73)

However, in spite of the consistent quality of naturalness
displayed by the characters in their conduct and conversation
and the astute observations of the author, Mrs. Barnes in this
novel never seems to have decided clearly whether she wanted
to write a comedy of manners or a serious study of the emotional difficulties of a woman approaching middle age; for, as
one reviewer observed, "In *Westward Passage* the author
achieves, perhaps less well than in *Years of Grace,* a natural
atmosphere drawn from clear observation of what people do
and say. The interpretation of how they feel, however, lying
just behind her words, lacks that inevitable accent without
which the rhythm of human lives seems somehow to have little
purport."[6] The feeling persists throughout this novel that Margaret Barnes was having a literary lark while she worked seriously upon the completion of her research for her third novel
Within This Present and that her uncertainty about her intent
and point of view weakens the novel. As a result, serious
moments in the novel are permitted to lapse into frothy
frivolity.

Nevertheless, despite the aura of triviality that pervades
much of *Westward Passage,* Margaret Barnes managed in her

delineation of Olivia to produce a portrait of unusual dimen-
sion. She viewed the dilemma of her heroine against the background of the social standards of the upper middle class in the
late nineteenth century. Olivia represents the typical socialite
of the period whose education extends only to the cultivation
of her good looks and charm in order to make an influential
marriage. Her inherent desire for adventure, combined with
her genuine interest in experiencing another kind of existence,
causes her to elope with Nick. However, with her very limited
social and intellectual horizon, she can neither understand nor
cope with his artistic temperament. But, when she marries
Harry, she responds perfectly to his desires and to the demands
of her position; yet, because she functions with such grace, she
believes she has lost all personal challenge. She knows that
she wants to experience in her life the same stimulation and
satisfaction that she realizes that Harry gains from a successful
venture in the stock market or that Nick receives from a favorable critical response to his latest novel. Olivia muses at the
outset of the crossing:

> Why, Olivia wondered, when you were embarking on a six days'
> voyage in a modern ocean liner equipped with a Ritz restaurant,
> did your loving friends and relations persist in sending you food?
> Food, which, being mortal, was destined to decay. It was, of course,
> a tradition surviving from a romantic past. A romantic past when
> an ocean voyage might prove really an adventure. When you sailed
> for a new world with high hopes of finding it—and were storm-tossed
> and ship-wrecked and—and got scurvy and *needed* a tangerine or
> a Hamburg grape, to help you swallow the salt pork. But nothing
> happened, nowadays, on an ocean liner. There were no new worlds
> to discover. (38)

Thus the voyage itself arouses Olivia's youthful longing for
adventure which she always associates with the bohemian set
on whose periphery she had lived during her first marriage.
Her particular mental state of dread causes her to blow their
achievements out of all reasonable proportion. She remembers
all of them as individuals of genius who have emerged as the
great pioneers in their chosen fields. Although there is nothing
to suggest that Nick is anything more than a successful author
whose work has received favorable critical response, she fancies

him to be a literary giant. She, too, as Nick's wife, once had
the opportunity to discover new worlds which she petulantly
threw away. And what has she accomplished as a result? Well,
she admits she has an unerring clothes sense and looks superbly
when dressed in the new fashions each season brings. As she
sees herself, she who could have been an explorer has turned
out to be a mannequin.

In this frame of mind, she views Nick's proposal as some
miraculous stroke of fortune that has intervened to give her
the second chance to attain her true potential. She returns to
him, only to suffer the shattering blow that neither he nor his
way of life can bring her anything but unhappiness. Finally, she
understands completely how false her illusions about her
talent have been. At last she truly appreciates how much
Harry's love means to her and is determined to make him as
good a wife as she possibly can. Nevertheless, there is the
matter of defeat which Olivia must accept. She must resign
herself to the clear fact that both emotionally and intellectually
she requires the security of the limited, patterned world of
fashionable society.

Therefore, if *Westward Passage* "has something of the fluffi-
ness of a strawberry soda, it also has something of the under-
lying tang."[7] This tang comes from Mrs. Barnes's treatment
of Olivia. She permitted no commentary by the author to creep
into the characterization. Olivia is known strictly through her
own expression of her thoughts, feelings, and impressions. This
technique slowly makes the reader aware that Olivia is a victim
of an intricately structured social system that securely, if decep-
ively, deprives the woman of any training that does not contribute to the creation of the lady and socialite. Olivia definitely
has ability; her ideas reflect discernment. Does she possess
sufficient talent to become the creative person she thinks she
wants to be? The only conclusion that the reader can draw is
that there is enough evidence to feel that she might have
attained that objective if social convention had not been
allowed to stunt her development. Margaret Barnes neatly
managed to convey her interpretation of "the poor little rich
girl."

CHAPTER *5*

Within This Present

MARGARET BARNES returned to the technique of the chronicle for *Within This Present* (1933) that she had used for *Years of Grace.*[1] In the preface, she expressed her gratitude for permission to research the files of the Chicago *Daily News* and the Chicago *Tribune;* and perhaps she wrote this novel more consciously as a social treatise than she did any of her other fiction. *Within This Present* recounts the history, as interpreted by Sally Sewall, of the wealthy, influential Sewalls of Chicago from the eve of World War I until the inauguration of President Franklin Roosevelt. On that fateful evening of June 28, 1914, the family gathers at the suburban estate of Horace Sewall to honor the seventieth birthday of the matriarch Sarah Baines Sewall, who with her now deceased husband had migrated to Chicago after the Civil War; lived through the Great Fire; and, as the city flourished, amassed a fortune in banking. By 1914, however, a sense of complacency has crept almost imperceptibly into the Sewall family; and this change in the family and in the times is indicated by Sally Sewall as she views the library in the Sewall mansion:

The lamp-lit room, the book-lined walls, the firelight glancing here and there on goldtooled bindings, soft music from the drawing-room—this after all was something to have achieved. And the family, itself—well-dressed, well-fed, amusing enough, always kind, usually courteous. . . . There was no place—there never would be—in this serene, safe room for the hardy pioneer virtues that have made it possible. The world had grown beyond them! "Other times, other customs."[2]

The Sewalls themselves complement this dignified, well-bred atmosphere: the hosts Evelyn and Horace, she from a

distinguished Philadelphia Quaker family who had met her
husband in her debut year and he an art connoisseur by personal choice but a banker by family tradition; and their two
children Sam, who attended Harvard, and Sally, who goes to
an eastern boarding school; Adelaide and Lambert, she the
daughter of an Episcopal bishop and he an Episcopal clergyman with a fashionable parish and their son Baines at Harvard;
Fred a handsome bachelor whose vocation is charming smart
dinner parties; Cora Sewall Truesdale and her husband George,
she a chic socialite and he an executive in the family bank
and their three children Cora and Kathleen at the same boarding school as Sally and Georgie, a boy of twelve.

The only outsiders at the party are Alan McLeod and his
children Alan, Jr., at Harvard and Rose, a debutante. McLeod,
a clever Scot, began as an office boy in the family bank and,
because of his uncanny business sense, has risen to direct the
financial policy. A long-time widower, he and his children
have become adopted members of the family. When, during
the course of the birthday dinner, Mr. McLeod raises the question of the possible repercussions from the assassination of the
Archduke Francis Ferdinand, his concern draws an instant
reaction:

"Oh, Mac!" cried Aunt Cora impatiently, "you're making a noise
like an Englishman! Last summer when we were over there—you
remember, George—the papers were full of fantastic fairy tales about
the inevitable German invasion."

"Well," Uncle Lambert was saying cheerfully . . . "I don't believe
in meddling with Europe and I don't agree with Mac. In the future
international difficulties will always be settled by arbitration. The
martial spirit is dead, thank God."

"Lambert," said Granny, "I wish you were right, but I think
you're wrong. The martial spirit is never dead. It sleeps through
fortunate generations; but it wakes up very quickly to the toot of
a fife. There's that roistering spirit in men which leads them to
think a good fight is a good lark—until they've been in one. And
the impulse to fight for your own incarnation of an ideal. I've seen
two wars start."

As she spoke, the young people began to sing. . . . Sally rose to
her feet. . . . She was not in the least interested in the way wars
started and the music was pulling her. . . . She had never seen
Cambridge, not yet New Haven, but she thanked God not one of

the family was a Yale man. Her thin little voice shrilled out suddenly in a transport of vicarious feeling. "Three cheers for Har-vard! And—Down with Yale!" (37–41)

I *End of an Era*

The younger generation of the Sewalls approaches the holo-caust of World War I with the same naïve intensity that it observes a Harvard-Yale football game. It supports the Allies passionately for exactly the same reasons it thanks God that no Yale man taints its ranks. But the war represents to it the opportunity to break away from established tradition. As Alan McLeod tells Sally Sewall, "I think a war would be the making of our generation, Sally. Something for us to accomplish. Some-thing our parents couldn't win for us. If *we* won it—us kids, I mean—we'd really feel we'd made a new world." (114) As might be expected, Sam and Alan immediately enlist upon the American declaration of war. Alan goes to Sally at her boarding school to ask her to marry him before he sails for France; and, caught in the emotion of the moment in addition to having always idealized him, Sally consents joyfully.

Despite wild parental protests about their youth or about Sally's not having made her debut, they are married and go to live in a boardinghouse near Fort Sheridan where Alan completes his training. Here they join Maisie and Avery Cald-well, whom they have known in Chicago, and meet Bee and Tim O'Hara from Waukegan, who have no social background and no independent income. For Sally, the O'Hara friendship proves a revelation; she finds Bee and Tim so much more inter-esting and congenial than Maisie and Avery because the O'Haras make her realize the narrowness of the prescribed circle in which she has existed.

The closer Sally grows to Bee, the more strongly she believes that the real value of the war lies in the fact that it will destroy the existing subtle, invisible, but strong social barriers. Even the death of her brother Sam in France does not shake her faith that, out of the destruction, a truly democratic society will emerge which will end intolerance and tyranny. She must admit, however, that the new world which Alan had prophesied would come in the aftermath of the war seems very remote to her. Then the thought flashes through her mind that, of course, when Alan returns, they will discover the way they together can best contribute to democratizing the social order. But Sally accepts this idea at best as sheer rationalization, for somehow her husband seems very much of a stranger to her—a feeling which alarms her profoundly when she considers their future.

When Alan returns from Europe, Sally meets him in New York. The impersonal surroundings of their suite at the Plaza Hotel accentuate their feeling of strangeness. When Alan pointedly asks her whether she would marry him now if they were not married,

The question startled Sally. Would she, she thought. Why, absurdly enough, of course she wouldn't! She would wait, she would see, she would try to find out what time and distance and war had done to both of them. She would take her time. But she could not say that to Alan.

"But—we *are* married," she protested.

"Yes, we are," said Alan. Then, very solemnly, "I thank God we are. Because, if we weren't, you know—perhaps we mightn't be. . . . I want so much to recapture what we had. . . . But tonight . . . I realized that—that, even so, things had happened to us. Things we hadn't shared. We were so young that we—we're different. We're shy with each other. We've got to begin all over again. That's—disconcerting. But Sally—I want you."

Presently.

"It—it *is* recaptured," whispered Sally. "This is just the same." But it was and it wasn't. Beyond her emotion, and curiously detached from it, Sally was thinking, "This is a different Alan. He's older—more serious. He's not a boy any longer." She did not yet feel quite married to him. . . . Then thought was submerged in feeling. The future was lost in the present. (231–33)

II   *The Aftermath of War*

Despite Alan's and Sally's genuine effort to recapture the past, they discover doing so to be increasingly difficult. Alan's war experience haunts him, and he tries desperately to convey something of his uncertainty about it and about the future:

"When you've started a war, you've simply got to win it. You can't afford to lose. But, my God! There are people here at home who think war's grand! Who think it's beautiful and heroic and—

and *right*. It's incredible. . . . Maybe we had to fight. I don't know.
It seemed as if we did. But it's done something to the fighters.
I didn't realize it until we came home. What was it all about, if
now we're going to go on just as we always have. . . . Why, I nearly
go crazy down there in the bank. They've forgotten the war—except
for the war debts. . . . I sound like a fool, I know, but I want something to live for. . . . I've got you, of course, Sally. But you're just
more me. I mean—we're one person. I think we both deserve something, after all we've been through. I know that sounds fatuous.
For in one way we don't. We're not important. But in another way,
we do because we're young and we—we *were* hopeful." (236–41)

Sally optimistically dismisses Alan's discontentment as the
mood of the moment. However, neither the birth of two sons
nor business success can any longer disguise their increasing
unhappiness. A sense of purposelessness engulfs Alan, for he
continues to find no challenge in banking yet can think of
nothing else that would interest him. He denounces the American smugness during the postwar years but makes no effort
to combat it; he merely attempts to relieve his frustration
through a constant search for excitement.

While Alan flounders aimlessly, Sally tries to come to grips
with the disintegration of their marriage. She has matured into
a bewildered young woman who cannot pinpoint the cause of
her bewilderment. Although she regrets sometimes that marriage interfered with her plans for college, she has no desire
for a career. She has never abandoned her intellectual interests,
but neither has she cultivated them. However, she understands
clearly that the war has wreaked more devastation than the
slaughter on the battlefields.

Sally sees her opinion about the impact of the war reaffirmed
in the difficulties of her cousins Cora and Kathleen Truesdale.
Tall, lanky, clever Cora despises the social whirl into which her
mother plunges her. Since the war made volunteer service fashionable, her mother encouraged her Red Cross work which
proved her executive ability. Cora, having always enjoyed
writing, begins seriously to work on a novel in the hope that
it will give her the opportunity to see if she can hold a job
in the literary field. However, the social outlook of her family
does not countenance a career other than marriage for women;
and she chafes under the yoke of luxurious enslavement. Cora

observes shrewdly, "I know exactly what I want to do, but mother won't let me do it. Maybe my own limitations wouldn't let me, either. But I'd like to find out. But, anyway, as long as I want to do it and keep on trying, I wouldn't call my state exactly boredom. Divine discontent—yes. I'm dreary and dejected and slightly dippy—but still often exhilarated."

Kathleen also falls prey to the social reaction to the war. At twenty-seven, she has changed from the dashing, ash-blonde beauty who entranced society as a debutante into a fascinating, sophisticated woman with whom the most eligible men fall in love. The ironic thing about Kathleen is that she very much desires to marry, and, from the worldly point of view, she has all of the most worthy candidates at her feet. However, she attaches little importance to money, social position, and business prospects of her suitors because none of them can offer her the challenge that she requires in marriage: "I'm bored to tears, all the time! What do I do—great grief—but look for excitement? I'll say I don't find it, but that's not because I have left a stone unturned. Here I am, twenty-seven years old, still knocking around the amateur bars of Chicago—just nine years older than I was when I took my first drink. . . . I often wonder myself, why I behave as well as I do. I want to get married, of course, but I don't see anyone around who seems to be worth marrying" (254–55). When Kathleen falls in love with Maurice Edelstein, a Jew from the Lower East Side of New York whose musical comedies have made him into the toast of Broadway, parental ostracism faces her if she marries him despite the sanctimonious pronouncement of her family that the war was a democratic crusade.

Outside the family circle, Sally observes the shattering effect of the war upon Bee and Tim O'Hara. When they move to Chicago where Tim rises rapidly as a bootlegger in the gang of Red Kelley, Sally cannot escape the fact that her friendship with them has had a great deal to do with driving Tim into gangsterism; for he is motivated by his desire that his family have the material advantages of the McLeods. When Tim is murdered in gang warfare, Bee says to Sally:

". . . the war killed Tim, as if he'd been killed in battle. If we'd never fought it, Tim would be living now. . . . But we did fight it, and it made him restless and discontented. And it brought prohibition and that brought the liquor traffic. It's all a piece of the same thing. If you want to reckon up the cost of war, you must count all the wrong it does, down the years—not just poor boys who died in the service. There's Sam . . . who gave his life for his country. But for one Sam, there's thousands of others who are walking the streets of the world. Men, married and single, rich and poor, whose chances were ruined by trouble that was none of their making. Most of them didn't even know it. Tim never did. Tim thought his life was grand." (362)

Nevertheless, in spite of the changes and the tragedy, Sally cannot deny the very positive results produced by the war. There is the case of Rose who served with the Red Cross in France, became engaged to a British officer who was killed, and bore out of wedlock his posthumous daughter Comfort, whom Chicago society accepts as her adopted war orphan. The war tested her character and standards to the hilt; yet she never wavered. Rose's ordeal has given her a strong social conscience and a desire to work for the alleviation of human ills. Fred Sewall's experience as an ambulance driver has transformed him from a charming man-about-town into one who has a keen concern about human problems and who notes a new strength emerging in the Sewall younger generation: "I shouldn't be surprised if we were quite a tough family—for all that for so many years we've had everything so soft. I can feel myself toughening, at any rate, as I grow older. It's very reassuring. And I can see a strain of toughness—oh, very definitely —coming out in each nephew and niece" (257).

If the war had developed an inner strength in those who fought in it, as Fred Sewall declares, it also had evoked an inspiring idealism in the youth, like Georgie Truesdale, who had lived through it. Georgie enters Harvard at the end of the war, and there the quest for internationalism dominates the intellectual atmosphere. He embraces socialism with youthful ardor; and, after his graduation, though he takes his place in the family bank, he spends his free time in volunteer work at Hull House. There he falls in love with Jean Howland, who resides at Hull House and who is a Vassar graduate and a doctoral candidate at the University of Chicago.

Since Georgie's parents refuse to tolerate his engagement—

primarily because of her family's friendship with too-liberal
Robert La Follette—Georgie prevails upon Sally to act as
chaperone for them on weekends. Sally appreciates Jean's intellectuality which never loses the light touch. Furthermore,
she admires the stimulus that they provide for each other and
recognizes that Jean's education and career make her a real
companion for Georgie. Sally views them "as belonging to
another generation—a younger, healthier, more rational one—a
generation untouched by the post-war hysteria" (349).

The superficial tranquility of the Sewall family crumbles when
Kathleen elopes with Maurice Edelstein. Although she took the
step very hesitantly because it would mean a complete break
with her parents, she never regrets her decision. In New York,
she gains new radiance in her happiness with Maurice; for
he, a very perceptive, sensitive man, has always understood
the quandary of Cora and of Kathleen. Through his personal
influence, he obtains a trial job for his sister-in-law on the
staff of *The New Yorker*. Defying her family, Cora accepts
the challenge and proves capable of winning a permanent
position with the magazine.

III   *Time of Decision*

The decisiveness of Sally's cousins prods her to come to
grips with her estrangement from Alan. In the throes of indecision
about what action to take, she hears the gossip that Alan loves
Maisie Caldwell, who she knows has ceased to care for Avery.
When this rumor crystallizes her unspoken fear that Alan
wants a divorce, she knows she must confront him directly.
When she does so, he admits he loves Maisie but denies she
had any part in the destruction of their marriage. To Alan, he
and Sally ". . . weren't ready for marriage. But the war came
along and it was like—a hot-house. It forced us into unnatural
bloom. You know what I mean. We *thought* we were ready.
. . . The first years we had—well, they were lovely. They were
lovely in a way that nothing can be again. But they couldn't
last. They were like a too early spring. And then—we grew up.
Up—and apart. And now, we're grown. We're a man and a
woman. We know we want—what we haven't had. And life's
slipping away from us" (429–31).

While Sally agrees with Alan's general analysis, she grasps the basic difference in their solution of the situation: she wants to recapture the past with him, but he desires a new future with Maisie. To Alan's consternation, Sally refuses to get a divorce. She explains that she and the boys will go to live in New York; then, after a year, he can divorce her upon the grounds of desertion if he still wishes to marry Maisie. When Sally departs, she is under the same cloud of family opposition that her cousins Cora and Kathleen had suffered.

In New York, Sally cultivates new facets of her personality in the company of the witty, intelligent, but thoroughly unconventional people with whom Kathleen and Cora consort. At first, Sally is dismayed that her cousins can cast aside so wholeheartedly the family propriety which has formed the cornerstone of their existence. However, the casualness of these new acquaintances appeals to her; and their conversation stimulates her to read voraciously, to visit all the galleries, and to attend concerts and theaters. Her critical judgment sharpens; it amazes and delights her to realize that clever, well-known people listen to her opinions. When she meets Oliver Wainwright, the son of a famous novelist and of a celebrated society beauty; a graduate of St. Mark's School, Yale; a Rhodes Scholar —who has chosen poetry for his vocation, he immediately fascinates Sally. His charm and decorum reflect her old world; his intellectuality and artistry enliven her new one. She responds to him with an intensity she never dreamed possible; but, when Oliver asks her to marry him, she feels his proposal to be a terrible threat to her internal security. Any thought of a decision about her future terrifies her. She knows that Oliver has a strong physical and intellectual attraction for her; yet she wonders whether, temperamentally, they could make each other happy if they should marry. There also remains the nagging fear that perhaps Alan is the only man whom she can truly love.

Although Sally has learned of Maisie's Paris divorce and subsequent marriage to a French nobleman, Alan has made no overtures toward a reconciliation. She realizes that, after her New York experience, she can never revert to the conventional pattern of her former life; even if Alan proposed a reconciliation, she recognizes that he might not care for the woman she has become. Moreover, marriage to Oliver poses grave questions for her too. She is aware of his uniqueness in the Edelstein circle; for, because of his financial independence, the reception of his poetry matters little to him. She misses, therefore, in Oliver the excitement of success she detects in Maurice; for, though Maurice sets the highest standards for himself, his critical and popular acclaim invigorates him. Perhaps, Sally feels, Oliver dismisses all success as vulgar; perhaps for this reason she considers him at times too effete and too much the dilettante. And she also considers the part she would play in Oliver's life and whether it would bring her true fulfillment. As his wife, she would face the challenge of catering to Oliver the poet and to Oliver the socialite; but Sally questions whether she possesses the special quality that Kathleen has of transforming a drawing room into a salon. When and if she remarries, she knows it must offer a vocation; for the onset of the Great Depression intensifies her desire to feel personally useful.

IV   *The Great Depression*

As Sally wrestles with her future, Fred Sewall arrives in New York to announce the delightful news of his engagement to Rose. At the family dinner of celebration, the conversation returns repeatedly to the implications of the depression. Fred declares he wishes everyone would adopt the positive attitude of his mother and of Georgie who conceive the depression to be a social war from which a more democratic, revitalized America will emerge. He believes that Jean and Georgie are discovering the same sense of achievement in relief work that he, Cora, and Rose had gained in the war:

Uncle Fred nodded, "I loved my ambulance. But perhaps—" His voice was a little doubtful.

"Perhaps what?" asked Sally.

"Perhaps," said Uncle Fred slowly, "it was just that I—I loved myself while I was running it. Do you know what I mean? I was doing something useful, for a change—"

"I know," broke in Cora. "Something useful and hard and brave and exciting. Something you were honestly convinced *ought* to be done. I felt just that way when the gobs got the flu and Mother thought I ought not to work with them and I did anyway. It's funny, isn't it?"

"What's funny?" asked Uncle Fred.

"That it takes a war to make us feel like that about working. I'm sure there's always that sort of work to be done. You might be running an ambulance now, for the County Hospital, and I might be slaving in soup-kitchens. The poor we have always with us. But we don't do it."

"Well, George *is* doing it. And Jean too. Granny says—"

"What does Granny say?" asked Sally.

"She says that in that sense the depression *is* a war, which will test the mettle of your generation. She says it's an emergency you all ought to rise to. She's very proud of Georgie."

"It seems to me that our generation has already had one war."

"Just the same, Sally," said Cora, "we didn't learn a thing by it. We risked our lives with pleasure, while it was going on. We really were selfless. A lot of us. Of course, we were young and foolish. But as soon as it was over we didn't give a damn. A damn, I mean, about what was happening to other people. Those gobs were a lot better off than most of the people in tenements. But I stood all night in the railroad yards, serving them coffee in the rain. I cried—I cried on curbstones when the doughboys marched past me. A lump came into my throat when I saw a waving flag. But a flag is only a symbol for the spirit of a nation. It ought to move us in peace, just as it does in war. We ought to march behind it to combat any evil. But we don't—" (489–90)

The tension mounts for Sally when she goes to Chicago for the wedding of Fred and Rose. She promises Oliver to return; however, when she learns of the imminent failure of the family bank, she knows she cannot expect either Alan or her father to support her in New York. Before the impact of the depression, Sally's thought of Oliver and marriage pales. Granny tells Sally: "I honestly believe . . . that this upheaval may be the making of my grandchildren, just the way those flames were the making of Chicago. We've lived in a wooden city. Our institutions weren't fireproof, and it's just as well that they should burn. Of course, I couldn't visualize the city of skyscrapers when I stood on the ashes of our house on Elm Street. But out of those ashes, the city came. You'll have to build the new world and I shan't live to see it. But I really have faith—" (578–79).

The bank disaster forces Sally and Alan to consider their future, and they decide to try a reconciliation. In returning to Alan, Sally experiences the feeling of useful vocation that she

has been seeking; for she and Alan must now work together if
they are to triumph over the crisis. She agrees with Granny that
the democratic society which the war promised but failed to
produce can evolve from having had to meet the challenge
presented by the financial panic.

The inauguration of Franklin Roosevelt confirms Sally's hope
about the future of America. Listening to the broadcast of his
inaugural address, the ringing conviction of his words thrills
her. Her father pronounces it the most stirring and eloquent
address since Woodrow Wilson, and Mr. McLeod adds: "You
can't help liking him. He's got so much nerve. There he stood
facing a complete breakdown of the national banking system—
and you heard the smile in his voice. You can't scare him with
any of the old bogies. He's like a little boy in the fairy tale,
who could neither shiver nor shake. He's got the country behind
him and four years ahead of him—eight probably—and they're
years in which anything can happen—" (606). Granny proclaims
the valedictory: "As I listened to that address, I was wishing
I could live forever. Something new is beginning. It makes me
think of the talk I used to hear in Chicago after the Great
Fire" (610).

V   An Interpretative History

In essence, Margaret Barnes wrote *Within This Present* as
an interpretive history of one segment of American society from
the outbreak of World War I to the onset of the Great
Depression.[3] Perhaps there can be detected in this novel a
stronger strain of didacticism than is evident in the rest of her
fiction which gives this work more of the overtones of a social
tract. However, this tractarian quality would have been much
more apparent at the time of publication since so much of the
subject matter was so extremely contemporary.[4] Perhaps the
passage of time has blunted some of the tractarian quality of
Within This Present; but it has not dulled the impact of the
dramatic irony that Mrs. Barnes achieved in the best of her
vignettes.

She depicted memorably the contrasting moods of jingoism
and the searching uncertainty existent in post-World War I
America in a conversation between Aunt Cora Truesdale and

Alan upon his return from service with the occupation forces in Germany.

"I can't get used to seeing you around here, Alan. It must seem nice to be home. . . . Those months in Germany must have been the last straw."

"They were, rather," said Alan. "They made you wonder what the war had been about."

"About?" said Aunt Cora sharply.

"Yes, the Germans in Marienthal didn't know—any more than we do here in Lakewood."

Aunt Cora frowned.

"I think we know well enough," she said. "We know that the Huns have menaced civilization since the dawn of history."

"When you see them," began Alan, "when you live with them—"

Aunt Cora interrupted him.

"Seeing isn't everything," she said decisively. "You didn't know what they were thinking. You couldn't talk to them."

"Oh, yes," said Alan mildly. "We could. We did."

"College German!" she said scornfully.

"College German, as far as I was concerned," he admitted. "But some of the Germans had relatives in America. . . . And lots of the enlisted men were German-Americans. . . . They spoke German like a mother tongue."

"Then they shouldn't have been sent to Germany," said Aunt Cora firmly. "I'm surprised there wasn't a mutiny in the ranks. It ought to be a lesson to us to stop immigration. This country is too easy going. America for the Americans!" With that, Aunt Cora moved off down the garden path. (236–37)

Sally, aware of how the conversation with Aunt Cora has disturbed Alan, questions him about his views; and he replies:

. . . I tell you, Sally, there's a gap between the point of view of the men who fought this war in France and the point of view of those who watched them do it. Of course, I didn't fight it. I only saw five days of action at the front. But I got to know the Rainbow Division pretty well and they'd been in it from the very start. When you fight a war, yourself, you don't try to justify it. You know it can't be justified. You know it's nothing more than a dirty job you have to do. But that doesn't make any difference. You're not there to know anything. You see ignorance and incompetence and mistakes in high quarters and discomfort and suffering and

death in loved ones. You see an amazing amount of courage everywhere. Just as you do in peace. But in war you're not supposed
to act on what you see. The only public virtue is to obey orders
and the only private one is not to behave like any kind of skunk. . . .
But I don't think the older generation can get away with raising all
that hell and telling us kids we were fighting to save humanity and
then expecting us to forget. Expecting us to be exactly the same.
The world can't open up and swallow the war as if it had slipped
into the crack of an earthquake. It won't stay swallowed. The earth
may quake again. (237–39)

Margaret Barnes caught equally effectively that strange combination of smugness, frustration, and idealism that characterized
the mind of the upper middle class American. Upon the announcement of the election of Herbert Hoover to the presidency,
the older generation of the Sewall family expresses relief about
the defeat of Alfred E. Smith because it means the preservation
of the American system of free enterprise. Alan protests
vehemently:

"Then, 'God's in his heaven, all's right with the world,'" he
remarked succinctly. "Well–I can't say that I care very much if
He and it are."
"Why not, son?" asked Mr. McLeod.
"Oh, hell!" remarked Alan profanely. "I don't know. Of course,
I'm perfectly sure, Dad, that you're right. You always are. But what
of it? That's what I want to know. Where's it all getting us? I know
I sound fit to be tied–but down there at the bank I just get fed
up with making money. . . . Where's the excitement?"
Granny looked critically at her grandson-in-law.
"Your father and Sally's grandfather, Alan," she observed with
some asperity, "didn't go into banking for excitement. . . . And money
was a by-product, too. . . . The Farmers' Loan and Trust Company
was more to your grandfather than just stone and mortar and it
was more than an opportunity to beat the market. It was a solid
foundation on which Chicago's progress and security could be built.
By serving it, he served his city. No one seems to feel like that
any longer about anything."
"I do, Granny," said Georgie very promptly. "I feel just that
way about the Socialist State."
Granny looked at him, very gravely and tenderly.
"But, Georgie," she said simply, "the Socialist State is non-
sensical. . . . But I've grown so old and I've seen so many changes

that I've almost come to feel that it doesn't make much difference *what* you believe in—the thing that's important is a state of belief. It's much better to believe in nonsense than in nothing, Georgie. In fact, it's often engaging. But when Alan stands there and tells us that all he wants out of life is excitement, well—I feel there's something definitely wrong with *him*." (252–54)

In another vein completely, Mrs. Barnes described amusingly and delightfully the upper middle class view of bohemian society through Sally's first impressions of the Edelstein salon:

Most of New York's celebrities seemed country-bred. Easterners, Westerners, Southerners, Gentiles and Jews—and twice the celebrity had been coloured—they had all drifted to Times Square, in some vaguely indefinite past, from smaller cities, country villages, isolated farmhouses, rural newspaper offices, Victorian homes, fresh-water colleges, busy factories, corner stores and in little red schoolhouses in the forty-eight States of the Union—human pollen, blown by the winds of doctrine to the Big City, to form there the floating intelligentsia which set the stamp of intelligence on New York. Sally had found them amusing, stimulating, and friendly, but a little bewildering. They were bolts from the blue. They had no background whatever, in the sense she defined background. (444)

In another accomplished vignette, Margaret Barnes pinpointed wonderfully the upper middle class psychological reaction to the Great Depression. To Cora's question of what exactly the failure of the Farmer's Loan and Trust Company would mean to the family, Sally answers that it is still too soon to tell. Cora inquires:

"Well ... do you think we're destitute?" Her tone was quite cheerful and curious.
"I don't know," said Sally, "but I doubt it. That seems, somehow unbelievable. People are never destitute." Cora laughed hollowly.
"Why, the flops are full of them."
"Well—not full of—of bankers. There's something very queer about the new poor. I've never understood it, Cora. You keep hearing of people who are utterly smashed, but the ones we know never seem to be reduced to anything worse than living in the old home on the Gold Coast with two servants. I could live like a queen with two servants. I did, all last winter, in New York."

"Yes—but we're casual. The older generation—well, you know how they are. Mother's definition of destitution would be a waitress who handed her a letter without a card tray under it...."

"Cora," she said musingly, "I don't suppose you remember something that Granny once said about us—long ago, when we were children. About all of us, I mean. She said we'd never known necessity.... I can remember thinking of Granny and of how she had lit into us. Thinking that she had a very exciting life. Really, you know, for the first time, that the call of necessity might be an adventure. I think this may be, Cora, before we're through with it." (570–73)

Within This Present represents a very ambitious effort to interpret contemporary American life as lived and understood by the upper middle class, and Mrs. Barnes succeeded admirably within the confines she set for herself. Her own firsthand knowledge of the world of Chicago society and the artistic scene of New York gave her a firm grasp of her material. While her prose is certainly not striking in any respect, her style is always literate, and the narrative flows easily.

The richness of her characterization is especially evident in this novel. She presented finely the shadings of difference in the outlooks between the various generations of the Sewalls. Moreover, the portraits of Bee and Tim O'Hara are consistent and excellent; they show that Margaret Barnes possessed the ability to move beyond the narrow orbit of the upper middle class.

A particularly interesting aspect of this novel is Mrs. Barnes's use of the Sewall family as a study of the leadership of the upper middle class. The matriarch Sarah Baines Sewall emphasizes that her husband never chose banking as a career to achieve personal success or to amass a fortune; rather, he viewed it as the best way he could contribute to the social progress of Chicago. She also stresses that the city would not have recovered from the Great Fire without the dedicated service of men and women who were willing to devote their leisure time to civic development. Thus, the men and women of this generation provided strong leadership, because they were deeply involved personally in public affairs and prized their ability to solve social problems.

This leadership falters with the second generation of the Sewalls. They develop a class consciousness, for they become aware that they are the socially elite. Their desire to retain their privileged position causes them to consider the preservation of social conventions more important than the commitment to social reform. No longer do their interests coincide with the interests of the community at large. They close their ranks by moving from the city to suburban estates. The sense of propriety guides their action. Horace Sewall, for example, assiduously carries out his duties at the bank and heads innumerable civic organizations; but his contribution is at best nominal since he does these things simply because it is expected of him. His real commitment is to the improvement of his art collection, which is entirely for his own enjoyment. His wife Evelyn, for all her Quaker principles, never publicly champions any cause. They have become too consciously genteel, and their one concern is to uphold the status of being cultured ladies and gentlemen.

Nevertheless, the complacency of the family cannot withstand the impact of World War I and the Great Depression. Mrs. Sewall feels the work of her grandson Georgie Truesdale reflects the emergence of a new spirit; her reaction to his activities is the key to Margaret Barnes's thesis. The old lady dismisses Georgie's ardent espousal of socialism as a fanciful dream, not from any attitude of political conservatism, but because she believes it represents impractical idealism. On the other hand, she warmly encourages his volunteer service among the unemployed at Hull House. The allusion to Hull House is very significant, for it was the remarkable accomplishment of Jane Addams that she created a dialogue between the classes and the masses in which social distinctions and political creeds were subordinated to community service. As Mrs. Sewall listens to her children's and grandchildren's discussion of Franklin Roosevelt's inaugural address, she remarks that their conversation recalls the vigorous cry for social reform that so inspired her generation in Chicago after the Great Fire.

The publication of *Within This Present* conclusively confirmed the talent of Margaret Barnes as an American chronicler.[5] In assessing the cumulative literary achievement of Mrs. Barnes, one critic observed: "The America in Mrs. Barnes' novels is more than mere background. In each of her works she is concerned with careful geographical and historical setting, but more important, she seeks in each character to find the essential qualities bred that mark him as that distinctive, if mixed character, an American. . . . Margaret Ayer Barnes tells us tales about ourselves, and who has ever been able to withstand the lure of his inimitable past?"[6]

Edna His Wife

MARGARET AYER BARNES continued in *Edna His Wife* (1935) to chronicle the course of American life during the first three decades of the twentieth century. In many respects, this third novel ranks as her best work, for it is a keenly perceptive, minutely detailed social history of the period. The chronicle centers on the marriage of Edna Looser and Paul Jones, who meet in 1900 when he is a bright, ambitious young lawyer; at the end of the novel, thirty-five years later, he has become one of the most eminent attorneys in the nation. Mrs. Barnes sets the scene with a fine introduction of Edna at the age of fifty-five in the prelude:

... a round little woman in the middle fifties, very carefully dressed in very obviously expensive clothes, so tight, so smooth, so plain, so serenely fitted over her plump contours, that they gave the impression that she must have been melted in some couturier's crucible and poured into them. Her "ensemble," as the couturier would have called it, was a symphony in black. The broad-tail collar of a black cloth coat fell open over her pouter-pigeon chest to reveal a black crepe gown and a decorous brooch of platinum-set diamonds, and a round black beret, adorned with a tiny eye veil, perched slantingly on the marcelled ripples of her blonde, bobbed hair. Her stubby feet were encased in black suède oxfords, her plump, short hands were moulded in black suède gloves. Black chiffon stockings, with distended clocks, stretching tightly over her insteps, struck a faintly lugubrious note and suggested that the round little woman might be in mourning. Beneath the small hat, her fat face— soft, mellow, smooth, and almost imperceptibly wrinkled around the eyes and double-chin line—had the texture and the colour of a slightly overripe apricot. It was a face that had been worked over for years by experienced operators in well-equipped beauty parlours.

91

Softened by creams, tightened by astringents, faintly tinged by rouge and dusted with the creamy bloom of Rachel powder, it would have presented an appearance as devoid of expression as the faces on the motion-picture "stills," except for the small pursed mouth that hinted of years of inarticulate suppressions, and the round blue eyes that held, at fifty-five, a vague look of almost girlish bewilderment, very incongruous and slightly ridiculous in that middle-aged face, but which somehow touched the heart.[1]

I *The Early Years*

The story of Edna and Paul unfolds through a series of flashbacks that follows the painful course of their life together from their first meeting, through their impossible married years as he rises to great public prominence and she futilely tries to adjust to their new position, and takes them to middle age where she seeks to discover how wealth can compensate for the loss of husband, children, family, and friends.

From their first meeting in the beer garden at Pinscher's Park in the little railroad junction of Blue Island, Illinois, Paul's compulsive drive for success has never ceased to bewilder her. Edna at twenty with her ash-blonde hair and china-blue eyes is the local belle whom everyone expects to marry promising Al Reimer, whom the town predicts will rise to the exalted position of head conductor on one of the transcontinental luxury trains. But, when she sets eyes on Paul, all thought of Al vanishes. To Edna, whose idea of taste is shaped by the popular magazines and Sunday supplements, Paul's dark good looks epitomize her ideal of the Gibson Man. However, upon closer acquaintance, she recognizes that "there was something hungry in the intentness of his dark, bright glance which suggested a nervous, exasperated power that she never detected in the illustrations of Charles Dana Gibson" (36). Her doll-like prettiness and rigid insistence upon social propriety amuse Paul; but he requests solemn permission to call upon her, her parents, and her sister Pearl.

During the initial stages of their courtship, Paul indulges in perfunctory flattery; later his conversation lapses into a monologue on law, on socialism, on Darwinism. Although Edna understands nothing and can think only of his handsomeness, she listens fascinatedly when he tells her about his early life in a Chicago orphanage; how he worked in the stockroom of a department store to earn money for his education and how his industry caught the attention of Mr. Steinmetz, an idealistic Jewish lawyer and instructor at Northwestern Law School; how Mr. Steinmetz encouraged him to go to law school; how he slaved to make top grades and simultaneously to make a living at odd-jobs and how finally Mr. Steinmetz offered him a position in his firm of Schutzberger, Steinmetz, and Stein. His unknown parentage and his saga enhance his romantic aura in Edna's eyes. They drift into a secret engagement that climaxes in an elopement when her parents refuse to allow her to marry a man of uncertain ancestry.

At first, Paul and Edna seem happy enough in their tiny Chicago apartment. Paul's life is his profession about which Edna comprehends nothing; nevertheless, he appreciates her domesticity and the very fact that he has a home for the first time. The birth of their daughter Jessie, a carbon copy of her father, delights them both. Although Paul's calculated ruthlessness in business dismays her, Edna enjoys his success and grows to like his benefactor Mr. Steinmetz and his wife. Indeed, her chief intellectual preoccupation becomes a thorough search of magazines and newspapers for recipes to tempt the Steinmetzs at their annual dinner party.

Upon the occasion of the fourth annual dinner party, Mr. Steinmetz informs Paul that he has been voted a partnership in the firm. Later, when the guests have departed and Edna expresses her pride in his promotion, Paul replies coldly that it will provide the stepping stone out of Schutzberger, Steinmetz, and Stein. His ingratitude and disloyalty to Mr. Steinmetz, to whom he owes everything, dumbfounds her. To her complete confusion, Paul continues his tirade by lashing out at his mentor's support of antitrust legislation:

I hope he'll shut up about it. Theories on social justice don't get you anywhere in the law. We're not legislators—we're not interested in changing times. The law's the law—and our business is to interpret it. Why, the Big Boys come to you, usually, to see how they can get around the laws we already have—with safety. They're a little careful how they express those sentiments, but that's what they really want. . . . Of course, Steinmetz is a college professor, at heart. He still gives those courses at Northwestern and he just loves them. They're a complete waste of time. He stands upon a rostrum and gasses away to a handful of idealistic kids and—well, it makes him impractical. (139–41)

As with most of Paul's outbursts, Edna does not attempt to grasp the essence of his meaning. She reflects vaguely upon his vehemence and concludes for the thousandth time that his childhood must have been very unhappy.

To do justice to Paul's new status, he tells Edna they must buy a house in the suburbs. Edna, always fearful of any change, has just begun to make acquaintances in the apartment house after their two-year residence. She tries to dissuade him; but she can never muster any argument that prevails against him. However, the eight years at Oakwood Terrace she remembers as her happiest ones. Here Paul, Jr., is born whom she hopes will forge a closer bond between Paul and her. She thrives in the folksiness of the neighborhood. Her feeling of triumph soars in 1910 when all the social leaders grace her tenth wedding anniversary tea, a feat that her friends assure her is unparalleled in the annals of Oakwood Terrace. Even Paul pronounces the occasion a success.

As they prepare for bed after the anniversary party, Paul, impressed by Edna's social success, makes a rare attempt to share his plans with her. He begins to explain the details of his current case, which, if he wins, it, will assure his inclusion in the ranks of Chicago's outstanding lawyers. Tired by the day's activity and unable to follow the intricate discussion, Edna climbs wearily into bed; instead of attentatively listening, she wonders how to turn the leftover cake into a dessert that will please the whole family. But Paul, in his excitement, continues to confide in her in a way he has seldom done even in the initial stages of their courtship:

"You see, Edna, ever since I was a kid, I've felt—I know—that a chance was all I needed. A break—that's all—"

But the confidence in his tone was oddly tempered by something boyish—something emotional—something strangely wistful. It was really as if he had turned to her for some note of reassurance and encouragement. But he did not get it.

"Edna?" Her name was no more than an incredible interrogation. He repeated it, breathlessly, "Edna?"

She did not answer. Then Paul laughed curtly and mirthlessly, and lay down again upon his pillow to plan for his future in silence.

For Edna was asleep. (178)

Paul's winning of his case gains him a partnership with Wintringham, Fox, and McElroy, the city's most distinguished firm. Although Edna is again disturbed by Paul's betrayal of Mr. Steinmetz, she becomes too elated about her friends' effusive congratulations and too apprehensive about Constance Wintringham's invitation to dinner to give much thought to her husband's unscrupulousness. For Paul, the Wintringham dinner is sheer delight; for a social challenge, like any other, exhilarates him. For Edna, so painfully aware of her own inadequacy, the evening is agonizing. When Paul questions her about her reaction, she hedges; then she blurts out that she would never feel at ease with these new women. He replies that she must make the effort, for he intends their children to move in the Wintringham social circle. Edna answers:

"But Paul—they couldn't."

"Why couldn't they? It's really very simple. It's merely a matter of neighbourhood and schools. Why shouldn't we get the best for them?"

"What is best?"

"Don't be silly. You know."

And Edna did. That was the odd thing about it. That is, perhaps, one of the odd things about American democracy. In spite of her affection for her friends on Oakwood Terrace and her liking for life there, and in spite of her own simplicity and her extreme discomfort that evening at dinner, Edna knew exactly what Paul meant. She believed there was a "best" and that the Wintringhams represented it. (217–18)

II *The Years of Success*

Thus, when Paul announces he has bought a house near the fashionable Wintringhams, Edna acquiesces submissively. She attempts to cope with her insecurity which neither the right dressmakers nor the most sought-after hairdressers can alleviate. The presence of servants terrifies her, so she delegates the running of the house to them. With Paul totally absorbed in

his law practice and with Jessie away at boarding school, Edna
in her loneliness turns for companionship to Junior, who is so
like her in temperament; but the strict regime prescribed by
his English nurse allows her little opportunity to see him.
However, the outbreak of World War I gives Edna a distinctive
identity for the first time. Her ability in rolling bandages and
her experience in knitting make her much in demand by
chairwomen of the various Allied relief committees. She loses
some of her shyness, and the other women view more appreci-
atively her homely talents. Upon America's declaration of war,
Paul informs her proudly that he has been summoned to
Washington as a consultant to the selective service system.

Although Edna has just begun to make a small place for
herself in Chicago, she never wavers in her determination to
establish a home for Paul in Washington. Much to her surprise,
she discovers she likes the capital; and, when Viola Sloane, the
wife of Paul's chief, calls, Edna hopes she has found a friend
in this member of an old New York family with a wide
Washington connection. Viola Sloane impresses Edna tremendously, and Edna understands the chic, the sophistication, and
the warmth of her guest; but Viola's intellectual curiosity and
her intense interest in political issues escape her. By the end
of the call, however, Edna realizes instinctively that Viola will
only receive her formally because of Paul. The exact reason
for her failure to establish contact puzzles Edna, for she senses
correctly that Viola cares nothing about the distance socially
that separates Blue Island from Park Avenue.

After Edna attends her first Sunday afternoon tea at the
Sloanes, she is even more baffled:

But she wondered . . . as she looked at the eager faces all around
her, why these people didn't seem to care about anything but talk.
The women's clothes were beautiful and the room looked lovely—
all firelight and flowers; the tea and the toast and little sponge
cakes were perfectly delicious. But no one seemed to be noticing
anything like that. All this casual luxury . . . was taken for granted,
as a background, a sounding board, against which conversation
ricocheted and reverberated, from the center of the government out
into the void. Nearly everyone was talking, intensively, fervently,
and those, who weren't, listening, passionately preoccupied apparently
with talk. Even Mrs. Sloane did not seem to be wondering, like

an ordinary hostess, if the tea was still hot, or if the next tray of
toast was coming in quickly. Edna had not heard anyone remark
upon the cake. It was really too delicious, she felt, to pass uncompli-
mented, but she did not feel equal to raising her voice in the din
that was around her. Paul's voice was raised. He was saying something clever about the cabinet and everyone was laughing. Edna
had not heard what it was. (316–17)

If the intellectual stimulus which the Sloane circle derives
from Washington does not register with Edna, neither does
the militant idealism of the government workers:

The most striking feature of the war emergency organization was
the faithful, unrecognized, unremunerated services of a myriad little
commonplace people who lived in wretched overcrowded boarding
houses, paying exorbitant prices for inadequate, often unsanitary
lodgings. Young girls left comfortable homes to accept voluntary
jobs under conditions that under normal circumstances, no paid office
assistant would for a moment tolerate. Middle-aged men left their
families behind, often in the most straitened circumstances, to lodge
themselves in wretched hall bedrooms and eat their hasty meals
off a counter at Child's. Married women cheerfully accepted the
curtailment of a bread-winner's income and shared the house of a
mother, mother-in-law, or sister in their home town, or, joined their
husbands, and, for the first time in their lives, cooked, cleaned and
even washed for a growing family. If a sense of adventure originally
lured these workers to Washington, certainly an acceptance of a
recognized obligation kept them there. (332)

For Edna, Washington exists only "as a sweet vernal
background for her private thoughts. Thoughts of the past and
of the present—and her first vague fear of the future, but
always a personal future. . . . The note of official governmental
administrative echoes or political uproar reached her but vaguely,
for it did not concern her. It had values for Paul, she knew,
but to her these values were never really clear" (327–28).   .
Even the influenza epidemic in 1918 does little to jar her out
of her private world. When Edna answers the urgent appeal for
volunteer nurses, she encounters "landladies too terrified to do
more than place a bottle of milk on the threshold of a sick-
room . . . double beds occupied by delirious girls. . . . One young
bride, hysterical with the fear of a possible miscarriage . . . a

boy, unconscious, died in her arms of double pneumonia before he had been seen by a doctor" (332–33). But none of these horrors really touches her; her deep reaction is her fear that she might contaminate Paul or Junior. The great satisfaction for her results from the knowledge that Paul approves of the course she has taken on her own initiative rather than from his suggestion.

With the announcement of the Armistice, Edna prepares the household for the eventual move back to Chicago; and she resolves to redouble her efforts to fit into the coterie Paul likes. As his associates depart and as his work slackens, he relies more on Edna's companionship; and she believes that they are at last achieving the closeness for which she has longed. Then, when he mentions in a quite off-hand fashion that he has accepted Arthur Sloane's offer of a partnership in his New York law firm, the news throws Edna into hysterics:

"Oh—I don't understand! How could you, Paul—how could you have all that on your mind—the way—the way we've been—and not even asking me—?"

"Not ask you what?" A conjugal patience veiled the weariness in his tone.

"If I wanted to—if I'd like it—if I thought it was the best thing for us! After all—it's my life, too. You treat me like an imbecile—"

"My dear Edna—"

The words were a bomb that burst at her feet. In the bright flash of the explosion, she saw the truth clearly.

"But I'm not!"

"You're not what?"

"Your dear Edna!" She was trembling with anger. Never before had she spoken like this to Paul. "I'm just your—oh God! What am I? I don't mean a thing to you, really. You go on—alone—in your own way—and you don't give a damn if I'm happy or unhappy! But I thought—I did think—that we'd come so close again—lately. Well—I see I was wrong."

"I'm not going to let you ruin my life," he said distinctly. "Not the children's lives, either. So you'll have to control yourself. I can't understand what all this shouting's for. There's nothing to row about. The Sloanes are delightful people and New York's a pleasant place to live in. . . . You can't make the charge that I'm not generous with you, Edna, and you'll have more money to play with than you've ever had before."

"I don't care about money!"

"Well, you spend it," observed Paul pleasantly. But perhaps his conscience pricked him, for he added: "And I like you to spend it. The children will love it."

"Oh, Paul—I can't—I can't bear it." Her voice was a wail of protest, but it held a note of resignation. She knew it would all happen, exactly as Paul planned. . . . "I don't mean a thing to him, really," she repeated in thought, very sadly. But still, they were married. And Edna was far too old-fashioned to admit the possibility that a husband might never, in one sense, come back to the wife at all. (347–49)

III *The Later Years*

As Edna had anticipated, loneliness keynotes her life in New York. Paul's legal practice absorbs him. The children treat her with affectionate indifference, for Jessie is now in a whirl as a debutante, and Junior is away at boarding school. The Sloanes maintain the same polite distance they did in Washington. Viola puts her on some volunteer boards; however, Edna recognizes she possesses neither the interest nor the ability to make any real contribution.

She resigns herself to the fact that "the mystery and wonder and joy in Paul's life were encompassed in four office walls" (403). Other women, she concludes with assurance, if they had existed, "they had never represented mystery and wonder and beauty and joy. If they had she would have known it. She would have read it in Paul's eyes, veil them as he would, some breathless sense of adventure. She would have resented it passionately. Curious that this sense of possession in a husband's happiness should linger so long after the possessor had been dispossessed" (*Ibid.*).

This belief in the physical possession of Paul becomes an obsession with her as her children thrust her more into the background. When Jessie announces her engagement to Dick Trevor, a brilliant medical student at Columbia's College of Physicians and Surgeons, Edna hopes fondly that the wedding preparations will draw her closer to her daughter. However, Jessie, who is like her father, knows exactly what she wants; and all her mother can do is to stand in awe of her executive ability. What means most to Edna is the visit of her sister Pearl and her brother-in-law Shoob, to whom Paul thoughtfully sends railroad tickets so they can attend the festivities.

After Jessie and Dick have left on their wedding trip, and while Junior and the rest of the bridal party continue the celebrations at nightclubs, Paul suggests they go to the theater:

That would be, thought Edna, as far as she was concerned, the perfect ironic ending for Jessie's wedding day. Junior off at the night clubs, and she and Paul sitting side by side, in speechless spiritual isolation, in a darkened theatre, with the garish stage-set of a musical comedy the incredible background for their parental hopes and fears. Hopes too divergent, fears too dissimilar, ever to be shared.

But Shoob's pale face had brightened and Pearl was beaming gratefully on her brother-in-law.

"Paul," she said warmly, "you're always thinking of someone else's pleasure."

Paul smiled like a Santa Claus. He had his small vanities, and showing off before Edna's family was still one of them. She could detect a faint glint of derision in his dark, bright eyes, but in spite of it she thought he looked as if he half believed Pearl's statement. (395)

If Edna only dimly appreciates Paul's intellectual prowess, he dismisses completely her intuitive shrewdness in dealing with Junior. At boarding school, their son excels in athletics and is voted the most popular boy in the class; but he displays no academic interests. She realizes he possesses neither his father's awesome drive nor his intellect; furthermore, she recognizes that, if Junior knew he had to earn his living, his outlook would change. Discussing his future with Paul, Edna asserts:

"I wish Junior had to earn his own living. Take some sort of a job."

"He couldn't hold it," said Paul. "His only hope is a sound college education."

"Oh," said Edna, "I don't mean that kind of a job at all. I mean—well, if it was different—if we were different—if we couldn't afford to educate him—why, he'd just have to do something. I'm sure there's something he could do. He—he could be an office boy—or mix sodas at a drugstore, or—"

"Would you like to see Junior mixing sodas?" Paul's voice rang with scorn.

She said slowly, "He wouldn't mix sodas forever, Paul. He'd—

somehow—get on. He'd get on if he had to—that's what I mean. Now, he knows it isn't necessary."

"But, my God, it is necessary!" cried Paul irascibly.

But Edna felt vaguely that he was missing the point. For Junior was a Looser, like his mother, like his grandfather. The world of Edna's childhood had been a small world of inglorious jobs and modest pleasures and sober thrifts and obscure destinies. Ambition and ability were rarely rewarded by more than adequate bread and butter. But boys made good in it, according to their lights. Junior would have fitted into that world, as he would never fit into the vast vista of his father's perspective. (399–400)

Paul, overriding Edna's opinion and the judgment of Junior's headmaster, insists that his son go to Harvard. Primarily out of fear of his father, Junior applies himself momentarily; and, by the narrowest margin, he passes his entrance examinations. At Harvard, however, he reverts to academic indolence and fails in his junior year, much to his father's fury and to his own disappointment, because he loves the life at college. Paul gets him a job in a Wall Street brokerage where he proves himself a born salesman, which enrages his father since it substantiates his mother's view about him. Junior escapes from a home made intolerable by his father's antagonism by eloping with Helen Cunningham of Providence, Rhode Island, a wealthy divorcée with two children.

With both children married, Paul decides to sell the large brownstone house and to move into a Park Avenue penthouse. Edna grows excited about the plan because she thinks it will give her something to do. However, Paul, without either considering or consulting her, seeks Jessie's aid in hiring professional decorators to redo the penthouse in an ultramodern style, which Edna neither understands nor likes. Edna, now fifty, takes stock of her situation:

What could she do? What was she fitted for? She asked herself these questions despairingly, and knew it was fantastic that no answer occurred to her. Of course, there was "charity." Edna blankly considered charity. She was still a member of the hospital and day nursery boards that ten years before, Viola Sloane had asked her to join. She went to their monthly meetings and listened to reports read by secretaries and treasurers and superintendents and matrons. She wrote out checks conscientiously, for their every appeal. She had served for ten years on the hospital linen committee. That was not very engrossing. For one year, she had made rather a hash of the job of corresponding secretary for the day nursery. She found note-writing hard. She thought she would enjoy some personal service with patients or the children, but both institutions were very well run by competent professionals who did not encourage sentimental board members to interfere with the routine. . . . But intimate relations were what Edna craved. She did not know how to achieve them outside the walls of her own household. . . . She had never met any of the husbands of the women who had served on the boards of the hospital and the day nursery. She had entered only a few of their houses. As a matter of fact, she had never entered any New York house, except in rare responses to a formal invitation. Not even Viola Sloane's. Viola and Arthur were kind, but in spite of that kindness, Edna had never penetrated the only intimate circle of whose existence she was aware in the entire city—the little group of people loosely classified as "old New Yorkers," whom the Sloanes had known for a lifetime. (454–59)

In her lonely idleness, Edna spends countless hours at Elizabeth Arden's where she meets Myrtle Throgmorton in an exercise class. Myrtle persuades her to join the dancing class of Prince Boris Dolokof, known to his intimates as Bobo. Bobo, good looking in a gigolo fashion, instantly appreciates the gullible vulnerability of Edna. She never doubts his tale of royal lineage and of his hair-raising escape from Bolshevik Russia, a story which varies with each recounting. After they have settled into the comfortable routine of lunching together, Bobo initiates the practice of dropping by the penthouse in the late afternoon for cocktails. When Edna feels she must confess her friendship with Bobo to Paul, he dismisses it with disinterested derision.

The flattering attention of Bobo touches Edna, but the amount of money he spends on her disturbs her. When she insists upon paying him a regular allowance, and he readily consents, an enchanted interlude begins for her, although she suffers pangs of conscience about her possible deception of Paul and about the number of large checks she writes. Her relationship culminates with Bobo when he professes his love for her and urges that they run away together. Edna, to his astonishment, answers that they must never see each other again; and, although he tries every means to break her resolve, she is firm. While she ultimately learns that he has gone off with another woman, nothing can destroy his magic for her:

> For a moment as brief as it was beautiful, the alchemy of love had transmuted the baser metal of her body into something desired and desirous. She felt herself a woman in a soft, sexual sense, as she had not felt for years. . . . She ignored her plump contours and remembered that a young man had loved her and found in that memory a pensive consolation. . . . She never distrusted the strength of the sincerity of Bobo's attachment, she thought sorrowfully, "He would have tired of me; he would have seen me grow old." Now she felt young, when she recalled his protestations. (502–3)

Edna gives up the appointments at Elizabeth Arden's since the sight of Myrtle Throgmorton evokes the image of Bobo too unbearably. With the birth of Jessie's son, knitting becomes her passion. When she can think of nothing else the baby needs, she uses the movies to fill the bleak hours; and she devours every detail she can read about her favorite stars. The only significance newspapers and magazines have for her is to provide additional tidbits to embellish her imaginary friendships. Into this fantasy world crashes the shattering news of Katherine Boyne.

Answering an urgent telephone call for Paul, she learns that a woman identified as Katherine Boyne has been critically injured by a taxicab and is asking insistently for her husband. Edna, believing her to be a client, gets in touch with Arthur Sloane, when Paul cannot be reached because he is on the golf course. Arthur's strange evasiveness and Edna's natural kindness prompt her to go to the hospital herself. Shortly afterward, when Paul arrives with Arthur, Edna grasps instinctively that Paul loves Katherine Boyne; and she leaves them together. Later that evening Arthur telephones Edna the news of Katherine's death. When Paul returns he tells her that he had met Katherine during his first year in New York, and he has loved her for fifteen years—and has done so without ever arousing Edna's suspicion. He is mildly surprised that her name means nothing to Edna because Katherine has won wide acclaim as a sculptor.

A greater sense of ignominy overwhelms Edna when she realizes that the Sloanes have approved tacitly of the affair: "It was not fair but it was so. On the whole, it seemed natural to Edna. She saw Katherine and Viola and Arthur in a little closed circle, around whose circumference she had hovered ineffectually. Seen thus, as a circle of four, it was not rimmed with passion, but with an even more insurmountable wall. Intellectual sympathy, mutual appreciation, charm and understanding. She had belonged outside of it. . . . She did not look at him, but said, 'I'm sorry.' She was not aware that in its simplicity this last observance had achieved dignity" (584–89). The knowledge of Katherine Boyne demolishes Edna's illusion about her possession of Paul, but she admits realistically that "bleakness was better than blindness" (607).

The bleakness for Edna climaxes with the death of Pearl, the only person whom she knows who truly cares about her. Returning from her sister's funeral in Chicago aboard the *Twentieth Century*, Edna recognizes Al Reimer, her former beau, as the Pullman conductor. They manage easily to push back the years, and Al impulsively invites her to dine with the train's crew. Her gaiety and warmth spark the dinner. Later, alone in her compartment, the memory of the evening plunges her into the depth of despair when she contrasts it with the life in New York to which she must return. She sees clearly that her future holds only increasing loneliness.

Wrench, the chauffeur, greets her at the station with the news that Paul has been called to Washington on business. As soon as she arrives at the penthouse, which she can never think of as home, she telephones Jessie in the hope that she might spend the day with her and the children. However, her daughter recites breathlessly her list of engagements, interspersing her recital with the information that she has sent the children out with their nurse. As the deathly emptiness of the penthouse closes in upon Edna, she realizes she must get out, do something to divert her from the recurring thought of Pearl which, in turn, makes her so painfully aware that she belongs nowhere. Edna, as she is introduced in the prelude, ponders what

. . . the distractions New York might offer, at that morning hour. Shopping?—there was nothing she needed. A facial and wave—the irony of that was too plain. She was unconscious of the deeper irony of the fact that nothing which the might and majesty of man had created or stored in that imperial city—save one thing [the movies]—could offer her the anodyne she was seeking.

Presently she walked out of the drawing-room and returned to
her bedroom and picked up her bedside telephone and dialed the
number of her garage.

By the time Wrench's voice answered her, she had conquered her
desperation and achieved a superficial tranquility.

There was nothing about her own voice that the chauffeur could
consider peculiar, as she said evenly, "I'm going out to the movies,
Wrench. Will you bring around the car?" (626–28)

Edna His Wife, which displays the talent of Margaret Barnes
as an American chronicler splendidly, is a fine, interpretive,
historical study of the first three decades of the twentieth
century. Mrs. Barnes covered a much wider social range in this
novel than she had in any of her other fiction, and the content
of the novel reflects her firm grasp of her chosen period. The
comparison and contrast of the social attitudes and codes of
behavior of these years is as important to the total success of
this work as is the story of the marriage of Edna and Paul Jones.
The journey of Edna and Paul from Blue Island, Illinois, to
New York wth the various stops along the way provides an
excellent opportunity to compare the views of the Looser household in small-town Blue Island with the attitudes of the middle
class suburbanites of Oak Terrace, then to consider the differences in the social codes of the upper middle class through the
Wintringham circle in Chicago and the Sloane salon in Washington and New York. Once again Mrs. Barnes re-created the changing tones of the era as well as depicted the feelings of her characters through elaborately detailed descriptions of décor. For
example, she emphasized the loneliness of Edna after the death
of Pearl through a fine description of Edna's entering the drawing room of her penthouse which she has never liked, nor has
she understood any of its artistic qualities:

Edna was standing on the drawing-room threshold, her eyes
wandering absently over its mist-grey walls; over the "eggplant"
curtains and the "oyster-white" upholstery, and the black marble
fireplace with its asymmetrical opening, and the Dufresne study of
zebras, and the white marble head of Brancusi, egg-shaped and
mournful, vaguely inclined in its posture of indefinite pain.

That head was, somehow, the last straw. Edna heard herself
laughing, softly, mirthlessly. "It's simply crazy," she thought, "that
I belong here. It's bewildering." (625)

Margaret Barnes produced two of her most striking and memorable portraits in the characterizations of Edna and Paul. She managed to remain rigidly impartial yet deeply sympathetic toward both of her protagonists which accounts for the excellence of their portrayal. In personality,

Edna was a purely emotional and imaginative person, and her imagination made up in intensity for what it lacked in range. Sometimes she felt fearfully that she only imagined the Paul Jones whom she hoped was her lover. For the mind behind his clever, sensitive face was a foreign country, which she was eager, yet powerless, to explore. . . . She respected tremendously the force of his intellect and she was always afraid that he was going to "see through her." For the Edna Paul Jones admired was not the Edna familiar from her babyhood to her father and her mother and Pearl. This was as near as she ever came to the definite realization that her whole attitude toward him was an elaborate, if unconscious, deception; a complicated pretence of interests utterly foreign to her nature, assumed in a passionate desire to please. Paul never really grasped the puzzled thoughts that were stumbling about her little blond head in the course of their long conversations. (58)

Mrs. Barnes developed her characterizations of Edna and Paul by concentrating on the intellectual abyss between them which widens steadily as the years pass. The evening of Paul's fiftieth birthday provides a deep insight into the outlooks of all of the members of the Jones family. Edna, who never loses a childlike love of any family celebration, plans a festive dinner to celebrate this milestone. However, on the birthday evening, she finds herself alone with the birthday cake when Paul telephones that he is too busy to come home to dinner. Jessie rushes in to say goodbye before going off to a debut party, and Junior is at boarding school. Edna, as she has done so many times, waits alone:

She heard downstairs the faint click of Paul's latchkey. She glanced at the clock and could hardly believe that it was twenty minutes to twelve. Well—the birthday wasn't quite over. Edna sprang to her feet and turned to the cake on the table beside and hastily scratched a match and began lighting the candles. . . . After a moment she heard Paul's feet on the stairs.

He saw the light . . . in the library . . . and [said] incredulously,
"Edna? Are you up?"

"Yes," she said, and went on hurriedly lighting the candles. All
but ten were burning, when he stood in the library door.

"Well—for heaven's sake!" he exclaimed.

"Happy birthday," said Edna. . . .

He smiled . . . and stooped to kiss her cheek and said, "Thank
you, my dear," very pleasantly.

Edna said, "There are your presents, Paul."

"Oh—" said Paul. . . .

They were Jessie's Charvet tie, and a tan Jaeger sweater, a pair
of black silk socks, and a Peck and Peck tie from Edna. Junior always
forgot all birthdays, except his own.

Paul unwrapped them . . . and said they were just what he needed.
Edna hoped he meant it. It was awfully hard to find presents for
Paul. When he wanted anything, he bought it. But the Charvet
tie was dashing—black China silk with orange and emerald-green
splotches. The kind of tie Edna never dared to buy. Sort of a
joke—but a joke in good taste. Her own tie was brown, with conservative tan stripes. . . .

Edna remarked, "You ought to wish and blow out your candles."

"All of them. . . . My wind's not up to it."

"Then we'll both blow," said Edna, "and I'll wish too."

So they stooped over the table and Edna tried to think quickly
of something nice to wish for. . . .She gasped at vague desire, and
thought inarticulately, "Oh—I—I'll wish him to be happy!"

Edna wondered what Paul had wished for. She had a silly feeling
that their wishes were in vain.

She said, however, "Now you must cut the cake," quite cheerfully.

"Cut it?" he questioned. His eyes had strayed to the clock
on the mantelpiece.

"Yes, cut it and eat it. Just two pieces—for luck, you know." A
note of apology was tempering the suggestion.

But he said, "All right," only a little uncertainly, and brightened,
as he added, "I think I'd like a highball."

That pleased Edna. "I'll get it for you," she said. "I'll have
one with you."

It was the work of five minutes to take the decanter of Scotch
whiskey from the sideboard and the glasses from the pantry and
to extricate the ice cubes from the ice box. She carried them upstairs
on the cocktail tray.

He . . . walked over to the table and poured two tall drinks.
He handed Edna her glass and raised his own and said, hopefully,
"Well—here's to the second half century."

Edna sipped the toast—she did not care much for whiskey—
reflecting that Paul's hope was probably well founded. The second
half century could hold a lot for a man. (369–77)

IV *Feminist Study*

In her portrait of Edna, Margaret Barnes accomplished a
particularly difficult literary feat by presenting the pathetic
plight of an extremely limited woman with a balance of irony
and sympathy.[2] Unlike any of the other women in Mrs. Barnes's
work, Edna totally lacks the ability to be able to rise to the
challenge forced upon her by Paul's success. Her doll-like prettiness, her sincere enthusiasm for pedestrian social functions, and
her unfailing kindness insure her a position in her own right
in the small-town environment of Blue Island or in the very
middle class, suburban atmosphere of Oakwood Terrace. However, when she must cope with being the wife of a public
figure, she fails because her honesty and her timidity always
hinder her from successfully playing the role in which she is
cast. She finds it impossible to disguise her disinterest in the
self-centered, insincere, fashionable women like Constance
Wintringham or in attending cocktail parties when she does not
like the taste of liquor. On the other hand, when she honestly
admires the social circle of the Sloanes and wants to join it, her
diffidence makes her appear more shallow, more inept, and more
boring than actually she is. The poignancy of Edna is derived
from the fact that she never deceives herself about her limitations and recognizes that she alone is responsible for her lonely,
futile existence. Sitting alone in a corner of Jessie's living room
at a dinner party,

She was well aware that Jessie was doing for Dick what she
had never done for Paul. Or for herself, for that matter. She admitted
that her social isolation was the result of her own temperament.
Still, you were as God made you. Edna sometimes wondered why
it had pleased Him in His wisdom, to make so many people dull.
Only the exceptions, really, were like Paul and Jessie. Yet they
always assumed that their stupid associates should be blamed for
their stupidity. Why? Edna wondered. It was a human quality,
like any other. Did stupidity do any more harm in the world than
cleverness? It was much less aggressive. Why must the stupid be

humble and accept a false hierarchy of interests that were foreign to their nature. Why should the clever impose on the stupid a standard of weights and measures that made them thoroughly uncomfortable? Tucked away in a corner, with her after-dinner coffee cup, Edna considered these questions dumbly, and never for an instant suspected in her humility that she might have advanced and defended them as a provocative sophistry that would have electrified the attention of a modern dinner party—a defence of the right to be dull. (412–13)

Another facet of Edna's character which underscores her touching but ironic position is her unflinching adherence to moral principle. After she refuses to elope with Bobo, she later reflects:

It did not occur to her to reconsider her decision, for she did not regard her action in dismissing Bobo as something she had decided. Choice had not operated. There was only one possible answer to his declaration. Edna still faced with the literal simplicity of Mrs. Looser the problem of "right and wrong." Doing right might make you miserable—it often did in fact—but doing wrong would not help matters. In affairs of the heart Edna's guileless judgment was unclouded by sophistry or sophistication. Nothing could make right an infatuation, an enchantment or a passion between a boy and a married woman. In all her confusion of heart and of intellect, that much was painfully plain. (502–3)

This simple, childlike moral stand of Edna prevents her from entering into an affair with Bobo that at least momentarily would have relieved some of her loneliness. In reality, her decision reveals to her how absolutely she is estranged from Paul and the world in which she now lives when she learns that Paul has deceived her in his love for Katherine Boyne and that the Sloanes have fully approved of their relationship.

While Mrs. Barnes never minimized the intense selfishness and intellectual arrogance of Paul, she caught equally the sense of frustration and the utter hopelessness he encounters in all his attempts to communicate his ideas to Edna, which accounts for much of his indifferent and often brutal treatment of her. Edna senses that Katherine Boyne's wide range of interests had attracted Paul and finally concludes that the intellectual alienation between them is too great ever to hope for even a remote reconciliation.

If Margaret Barnes refrained from passing judgment on the characters of Edna and Paul, she indicted the social system that shaped them. The feeling prevails throughout the novel that Mrs. Barnes intended it to read as a feminist tract as well as a work of fiction. She closely examined those social factors that influenced the development of Edna and the other women who have any real association with her. The analyses of these women with wide temperamental differences and from very diversified backgrounds demonstrate the importance of work to their fulfillment as human beings. Margaret Barnes did not necessarily interpret work as the active pursuit of a career but considered that women required the opportunity to engage in meaningful activity outside of the traditional realm of the home. Her ironic subtitle *An American Idyll* seems to reinforce the idea of the novel as a feminist study.

Of the women of Edna's generation, only Viola Sloane and Katherine Boyne experience complete happiness and true personal fulfillment. They do so because they recognize the necessity of bringing both love and purpose into their lives. Viola Sloane achieves this goal as the helpmate and companion of her husband, and together they provide the stimulating leadership for their influential salon. Katherine Boyne, too, accomplishes the same objective through her sculpture and liaison with Paul. These women not only give happiness; they also contribute to the betterment of human society.

On the other hand, Edna and the society women in the circle of Constance Wintringham offer very little to their marriages, and they contribute nothing of value. Although the Wintringham set displays caustic wit and brittle sophistication, none of them shows Edna's pathetic, ineffectual desire to serve. Constance Wintringham shuns all responsibilities by indulging herself in periodic "breakdowns" which require long visits to lavish, exclusive sanitariums.

Margaret Barnes dismissed women like Constance Wintringham with sharp sarcasm because they had the ability and the opportunity to be Viola Sloanes if they chose to be. Furthermore, the snobbishness of the Wintringham circle means that the only influence they exert is on each other. If they all decide to follow Constance Wintringham's example of going to expensive sanitariums, they are no loss to anyone.

However, Mrs. Barnes saw the pathetic circumstances of the woman like Edna who is trapped by tradition. As a man, Paul receives all the incentive and encouragement he needs to succeed in his rise from a Chicago orphanage to a partnership in an outstanding New York law firm. American tradition reveres the idea of the self-made man. However, Edna, regardless of her potential, has none of Paul's opportunities because the whole society, which includes women, deliberately conspires to close the avenues for self-advancement to the average woman. Only women of exceptional talent like Katherine Boyne or intellectual women of wealth and social position like Viola Sloane can hope to overcome the traditional antipathy to any feminist ideology.

Edna's unfortunate failure is the result of the American traditional hostility to the idea of the self-made woman, which springs from the firm belief that feminine activity must be restricted to the home. It is possible that, if Edna in her youth had been encouraged to broaden her interests or even if she had received at the outset of Paul's success some real assistance from a person like Constance Wintringham, she might have developed into quite a different person. She realizes she has failed Paul and understands that the Sloanes have accepted Katherine Boyne because of her own shortcomings. Moreover, she recognizes that the successful life of Jessie results largely from the example of Viola Sloane. Her daughter, to Edna's great admiration, manages to take an active part in civic affairs through her volunteer work with the Junior League, to become a discriminating patron of the arts, and to be a fine wife and mother.

Edna His Wife represents Mrs. Barnes's most ambitious literary effort. Her characterization of Edna is a memorable one. As a chronicle of American life, the novel is astute and re-creates vividly the mood and mores of the early twentieth century.

CHAPTER 7

Wisdom's Gate

M ARGARET BARNES'S last novel lacks the authority of her best work. Although *Wisdom's Gate* (1938) continues the experiences of characters in *Years of Grace* and *Within This Present*, it does not represent in the strictest sense a sequel to either novel. Instead, Mrs. Barnes used these familiar figures to explore the impact of the Jazz Age of the 1920's and the Great Depression and its aftermath of the 1930's upon the generation who had grown up during the era of World War I.

I Cicily and Albert Lancaster

Wisdom's Gate focuses on the marriage of Cicily Carver and her second husband Albert Lancaster. The combination of financial uncertainty in the years following the Great Depression and of Albert's indiscreet flirtation with the wife of the British minister in Shanghai forces Albert to resign from the foreign-service and to accept a job in stepfather Ed Brown's Chicago advertising agency. Both of the Lancasters regret the necessity of the move, for neither relishes the return to the conventionality of American surburban life. Cicily, in particular, has great apprehension about living in the same house and locale of her first marriage. She recognizes, however, that she must face the challenge of continuing her present life with the constant encroachment of the past. Everywhere she encounters the specter of her divorced husband Jack which recalls his blind devotion and the unclouded innocence of their happiness.

She uneasily admits that "the broken threads of the earlier, more artless adventure of her girlhood stood out, patched and frayed in the texture of her life, which Cicily would have liked to see as an unbroken pattern, illustrating the theme of a

112

single devotion. She could not, for she had loved Jack—or had thought she had loved him. But never as I love Albert, she told herself. That was not quite true, and she was dimly aware of it."[1]

Her perplexity about herself mounts as she realizes she possessed a desirability for Albert as Jack's wife which somehow she has lost as his wife. Albert, handsome, suave, intelligent, radiates a charm that few people can resist. However, as Cicily has experienced, the grind of what he regards as boring routine makes him petulant, temperamental, and wayward. He grates under the prescribed ritual of the business world and suburban life, so he searches for distraction. He finds it in Gertrude Sewall, the chic, amusing, divorced wife of Baines Sewall. Gertrude inflames his ego but does it in such an expert yet seemingly languid fashion that her every move intrigues him. Cicily senses that the greatest pleasure they derive from their flirtation is the gossip they inspire. As Albert explains to Cicily,

Darling, we live in a complicated world and we're going to live in it for a long time together. We mustn't allow ourselves to be destroyed by complications, for we can't avoid them. . . . But there's nothing complex about our relation to each other. That's as simple as it ever was and grows stronger with time. . . . There's so much that's dreary in life. . . . I am entertained by women. I have always been. But, sweet, is it so serious? Why shouldn't we pick up a little fun where we find it, as long as we relate it, in the proper proportion, to the things that *do* matter? It's so insignificant that it has no bearing on them. It's on another plane. (137–41)

Albert's ingenuous frankness counters any rebuttal Cicily might muster; but she cannot escape the conclusion that his naïve sincerity poses a possible threat to their marriage. On one hand, she sees clearly that, if she satisfied him completely, he would have no interest in any other women; on the other hand, she questions seriously whether any woman can maintain the illusion of fascination sufficient to hold a man like Albert. In any case, her uncertainty about her relationship with Albert plagues Cicily. When her children hear that their father Jack is to remarry, they ask their mother about the reasons for their parents' divorce. In formulating her explanation, she analyzes carefully her own feeling about herself and the past:

"Nothing ever happened that you shouldn't hear about. There's nothing I could say to you in criticism of your father. I can tell you truly that he was good and kind. He was better than I was, more faithful, steadier." This much justice demanded. Still, she felt heartened by her own magnanimity. She essayed a faint smile. "But I somehow stopped loving him. That, I really can't explain to you. Love—" She paused helplessly, floored by the word, meeting the stare of their intent young eyes. "Well, it's a mystery," she went on tritely. "It comes and goes. You can't make yourself love anyone—or keep yourself from it. I always—through it all—liked your father tremendously. I respected and admired him." How ridiculous words were! How inadequate, cold. *Liked* Jack? She'd loved him—though not as she should—she'd pitied him, grieved for him—"But that's not enough," she heard herself saying, "and because it isn't, you become nervously irritated by so many little things. And then, I was not in love and very unhappy. For love is—it can be—the most beautiful companion. When it leaves you, you find you are very much alone. I was twenty-eight years old and I couldn't quite face . . . a life that was loveless." Then she pulled herself up and thought, oh, how mawkish! I mustn't sentimentalize and play on their sympathies. And it wasn't like that—so sweet and grave. It was terribly tedious. She added abruptly, "I was very bored." (150–53)

Her last remark takes the children aback, and they look shocked; and she realizes that she should never have spoken so bluntly. Their sense of romance irritates her, but she calms herself with the thought that age and experience will temper their romanticism. Nevertheless, the feeling that her hasty, tactless statement might either disillusion them or unhinge their trust in her upsets her; as she continues, she therefore weighs her words carefully:

"Then your Uncle Albert came back from Europe." This twist of the plot must be delicately handled. "Of course he was married to your Aunt Belle. They hadn't been happy and he—he fell in love with me." So she put it quite bluntly. "I'm afraid, at your age, you'll find that hard to understand. You'll have to take my word for it and also for the fact that when I knew—when he told me"—here her voice dropped and faltered—"it changed the whole world for me. . . . Darling children . . . this you *must* understand. Love commands respect, wherever it exists; in itself it is beautiful and it's wrong to deny it." That was the creed impressed on her by Albert, on which she had acted. But thinking of Albert, she added as an afterthought, "When it's real love, that is," and realized instantly that her appeal had been weakened by this qualification and wished that she had omitted it. . . . She thought for some moments, with increasing bewilderment, of all she had said and of how they had listened to it and of what she had done. What she had done was a very old story, but it had taken on freshness and colour and poignancy from the reactions of the children who had just heard it.

"Tout comprendre, c'est tout pardonner"—she had always believed and quoted that proverb. If you could explain, your critics would be disarmed. For the first time she doubted it. What you explained was the thing that was significant. It might, or might not, seem worthy of approval. (155–58)

II *Cicily's Dilemma*

The test of Cicily's belief in her unshakable love for Albert comes when she learns that he faces a pending lawsuit for alienation of affection. Albert's secretary Miss Sadie, an elderly spinster who worships him, finally musters the courage to tell her that Ivy Doty, a former Miss Wisconsin and a model at the agency, has left her husband and that he has retaliated by naming Albert as corespondent. The information shatters Cicily's composure; for, since Albert kept her in total ignorance about the situation, the news confirms so many of her unspoken fears about the jeopardy of her marriage.

When Cicily confronts Albert directly and begs for the truth, he explains away the affair in such a plausible fashion that even Cicily begins to believe that he is an innocent victim of his own charm. He convinces her that he had no inkling that Ivy had fallen in love with him and that her unscrupulous husband had taken advantage of her confession to extract twenty-five thousand dollars from him or to force him to face a scandal which would end forever all hope of his returning to the foreign service. Cicily, who agrees that there must be no lawsuit, volunteers to sell some of her stock in the Carver bank to cover the price demanded by the irate husband.

However, an unexpected, early morning visit from her mother-in-law, the Aunt Muriel of her youth, renews Cicily's suspicion. Aunt Muriel opens the conversation smoothly: "Cicily . . . if you were my own daughter, I couldn't be fonder of you. . . . You have been, and are, a perfect wife for Albert.... This has made me very happy. I hope you realize that he really adores you and that I am grateful for—for your qualities of character. I think you understand him and—" (186–87).

Unable to cope with her mother-in-law's subtle hedging, Cicily interrupts to inform her that she and Albert have always had a perfect understanding based upon their belief in complete frankness with each other. She notices that the emphasis she placed on the phrase "complete frankness" silences Aunt Muriel, and she watches her mother-in-law mentally shift her strategy. Cicily also sees that the anxiety and the tension have made her mother-in-law appear to be for the first time an older woman. Slowly Aunt Muriel begins again; but her daughter-in-law, hoping to avoid an emotional scene, replies curtly that Albert has told her all about the Doty suit; they have discussed the unfortunate situation from every angle; and, for the good of all concerned, they have reached a complete agreement that there must be no scandal. Aunt Muriel, aghast, cries out softly:

"And you—Cicily, darling... you mean you've forgiven him?"
The phrase was pure melodrama, Cicily thought. And it voiced a curiosity that she could not condone. "Of course I've forgiven him. Don't I have to? You know Albert. He goes down like a nine pin before a pretty girl. He and Miss Wisconsin—well, it's really too ridiculous to take very seriously. Of course, I don't like it. I wish it hadn't happened. It's going to be very expensive. But at least it's over. He really regrets it." After an instant of blank, dazed silence, "I had no idea that you were such a realist, Cicily," her mother-in-law observed in a queer, dry tone.
The queerness snagged Cicily's attention unpleasantly. Something not understood had arisen between them. She asked, "What do you mean...."
"I mean, my dear child, that you're right but remarkable. I didn't expect you'd be so wise. At your age, I'm sure, I didn't have half your composure. But we took sex more seriously. And much more romantically. Whether, my dear, we were deceived or deceiving.... But men and women were, of course, just the same. Such escapades are always superficial, and a wife, if she's sensible, always wins in the enu. If she's pretty, that is, and thinks it worthwhile. For Albert, my dear child, is simply devoted to you. He told me so yesterday with tears in his eyes. But don't think I'm trying to excuse his

conduct. I think it was disgraceful. To forget you—and himself—
to have an affair with a model in Ed's office—" Her voice sank
disdainfully. (188–89)

Cicily, incredulous, stares blankly at her mother-in-law. She
appears not to have comprehended anything that Aunt Muriel
has said. Finally Cicily manages to mumble something incom-
prehensible about Albert's having had an affair:

"Oh, my dear, it was that!" cried Aunt Muriel quickly. Her
accent was curiously that of reassurance. "You couldn't call it seduc-
tion, as Doty pretends. She was an experienced married woman and
she knew what was happening quite as well as Albert did. She
admits it, in fact ... Doty's behaviour has utterly outraged her.
I saw her yesterday. ... I must say ... she behaved very well. She
was quiet and dignified and said, rather courageously, that if it
weren't for this action that her husband insists on she wouldn't
regret anything. She said she was willing to write it off to experience.
That seemed a trifle hard. But she thinks only of Albert and seems
perfectly reconciled to fading out of the picture. I think, from the
first, she knew that was inevitable." (189–90)

Once more Cicily gazes in disbelief at Aunt Muriel, whose
courageous realism she admires; but now the very sound of
Ivy Doty's name fills her with revulsion. She wonders if she
can hide from her sympathetic mother-in-law the horrible
knowledge that Albert has lied to her, that he has employed
every deceitful trick to mislead her, and that she has believed
and trusted him. Aunt Muriel watches her silently, then asks
quietly:

"Have you decided ... you and Albert, I mean, what you are
going to do?"
"Do?"
"About Doty," said Aunt Muriel.
"Oh, Doty," said Cicily, as queerly and listlessly as if her wits
were wandering. The name seemed to come to her from very far
away. But it brought with it the vulgarity of the courtroom. ... Her
[Cicily] sense of shame of it was horribly intensified by the knowl-
edge that Doty was honest and just. ...
"Oh, I guess we'll have to settle," she said apathetically.
"You mean—?" Aunt Muriel was suddenly eager. ...

Aloud, she said savagely, "I mean that I'll pay," and glared at her mother-in-law.

Aunt Muriel looked very grateful for the glare. . . . She had grown a little older, or so Cicily fancied, in the dreadful half-hour that they had just put behind them. But she was recovering, as Albert could recover, from any experience, from any shattering blow. Sunny was the word for it—a sunny nature. She rose from the sofa and stood smiling beatifically, all of her gratitude shining in her eyes. (191–92)

As Aunt Muriel prepares to depart, Cicily catches the glowering reflection of Albert in the mirror. She lets her eyes drift to a letter addressed to Alden Carver, her uncle in Boston, who handles her trust fund. Albert, sensing that she knows the truth, watches anxiously to see what she will do. Cicily hands the letter to her mother-in-law with the request to post it in town so that it will make the afternoon mail:

Aunt Muriel, too, observed the name and the address. She was somewhat deficient in small, personal decencies and would always glance curiously at a letter in her hand. The four lines of script in Cicily's square handwriting—which always looked so childish— seemed to move her profoundly. "Oh—Cicily—" she stammered. And burst into tears.

She knows what it means, thought Cicily dully, as she patted the mink on Aunt Muriel's shoulder. . . . The tears subsided and the damage was repaired—with a thought for the chauffeur who was waiting in the limousine—with powder and mirror. (196)

When Albert tries desperately to reason with Cicily about his lack of honesty, he argues that, if he had told her the truth, he would have forced her to assume a responsibility which should be his alone. She informs him icily that the only reality to her is that her husband not only had committed adultery but had also lied to her about it. Albert, finally aware that he cannot rationalize his behavior to her, observes with ruthless honesty: "Wives, as a rule—sweet wives, like you— are relatively immune or else not exposed to that sort of temptation. But a very good husband can think—it would be fun. It *is* fun, damn it! You can't get away from it. But it never touched my deep feeling for you. Of course, it sometimes troubled me, but I though you'd never know and no harm

would be done. That's the absolute truth and you see you
don't like it" (199–200).

III   *Cicily's Solution*

The crisis provides Cicily with acute insight into Albert's
character and his view of life, which she had never before
grasped so clearly. Nevertheless, this knowledge resolves nothing
for her. She feels that she cannot continue to live as his wife;
but, since she cannot bear to admit a second marital failure,
the thought of divorce terrifies her. Her ultimate solution rests
upon the precarious assumption that she and Albert can go
their separate ways and yet maintain appearances by existing
together in harmony.

Throughout her daughter's unhappy trial, Jane Carver has
observed the developments carefully and has pondered the
alternatives; but she has refused to intervene except to prevail
upon Stephen not to push Cicily into divorce. She knows only
too well the dangers of unsolicited advice. However, Cicily in
her indecision turns to her mother:

"Really, I haven't a notion what to do. Often it seems nothing
right can be done."

"Right?" Jane's irony was barely perceptible. "That's an old-
fashioned word, my dear. I wasn't going to mention rightness and
wrongness. I know you think them both a matter of opinion."

"No, I don't, Mumsy." But Cicily could remember that when
she'd left Jack she'd turned a deaf ear on moral abstractions. "Only
it's complicated. I think it's hard to generalize. Sometimes the right
is a mere choice of evils. But I really believe in a given situation,
you're dimly aware of what seems to be most decent. . . . I suppose
that monogamy is the really right idea—when children are concerned. But it's often impractical!"

"Isn't the alternative?"

Cicily stared. God knew it was! She felt her last remark had
been childish and trivial. Her mother's simplicity seemed the ultimate
sophistication. Aloud, she admitted, "I think it is, Mumsy. It seems
to me that my generation has had to learn by experience while you
knew by instinct."

Jane, for an instant, looked slightly amused. "We had our
experiences."

"But you weathered them." (340–41)

Jane hesitates, reflecting whether the time has come when she can speak her views frankly about the course her daughter has chosen to pursue. She feels her way somewhat tentatively, then launches a direct attack:

"Cicily ... don't think I don't know what you've had to put up with. But have you, of late, given Albert a fair deal?"

"That," said Cicily coldly, "doesn't make any difference. No matter what deal he has—"

Jane murmured, "I know." She faced the dilemma for an instant in silence. Then, as one who neither minimized nor exaggerated its difficulties said philosophically, "He doesn't attach much importance to it [adultery], Cicily."

"I do."

"Of course. So do all women. But to some men, my child, physical infidelity is strangely immaterial. It has little bearing on their permanent affections."

"Those men shouldn't marry."

"They usually do, dear—again and again. As often as their wives decide they can't bear it. . . ."

"Well, I have decided," she said with determination. "I know you hate the very thought of divorce. You're thinking of the children—"

"No," said Jane unexpectedly, "would you be happier without him ... I think it's your misfortune to love him. . . . If you'll face that fact, you'll find everything's simplified."

Cicily ... said, her voice trembling, "Suspicion destroys love. And I have to suspect. I'd be a fool not to. . . ."

"On the contrary, Cicily, I think you'd be wise."

"You mean—shut my eyes? Mumsy, I can't. . . . I only want peace." She almost believed it.

"They used to tell us—I mean my generation—nothing can bring you peace but a triumph of principle," said Jane, not sententiously, rather, indeed, with a tender humour, an accent of quotation making light of the phrase.

"Then perhaps I'll achieve it," said Cicily, thinking. (341–43)

Slowly Cicily grasps the subtlety of her mother's point of view. Although she knows her mother's fondness for the New England Transcendentalists, she recognizes that the force of "principle" to Jane does not mean some murky, moral idealism or an existence dedicated to some noble, lofty cause. Rather, Cicily interprets it to mean the achievement of a direction in life instead of an aimless drifting. As Jane has perceived clearly, Cicily can find no lasting happiness without Albert. Her love for him, despite everything he has done or anything he will do, will always remain the focal point of her existence. To leave Albert would mean the destruction of herself.

Having accepted her vital need of Albert, Cicily comes to understand the intensity of his feeling about her. Aunt Muriel, after much clever maneuvering, persuades Ed Brown to settle enough money on Albert so that he can return to the foreign-service. When Albert begs Cicily to go with him, he tells her simply that personally he can imagine no future without her and that her charm, poise, and adaptability mean everything to his success as a diplomat. When she seems to waver Albert pleads: "Because I've been a rotten husband, you think I don't love you. But for once you're wrong, Cicily. You're the solidest thing in my life. And the dearest" (363).

His words recall her conversation with her mother. His straightforward emphasis on her being "the solidest thing" in his life convinces her that he does care for her and over-comes any resistance she might have shown. Cicily knows that, if she can offer Albert the stability he requires, she will have gained "the triumph of principle" she has sought. However, she holds no illusions about her future: "'Dearest and solidest' —well, wasn't that enough? There would be others less solid, less dear. She faced that fact, helplessly.... She would have to put up with it..." (364).

IV *Portraits of an Era*

Wisdom's Gate certainly does not have the stature of the best fiction of Margaret Barnes. Although the novel offers an always perceptive and often provocative commentary on some aspects of American life, the individual vignette stands out rather than the work as an integrated whole. This factor weakens the novel structurally, for too often it disintegrates into a series of episodes very loosely spliced together. Nevertheless, in many of the incidents, Mrs. Barnes caught effectively and accurately the unsettled, anxious mood of the American upper middle class in the wake of the Great War and the Great Depression.

Despite the limitations of the novel, Margaret Barnes did

manage to dramatize the marital problems of Cicily and
Albert.[2] In light of the restraint of the fiction of her era, her
frank treatment of sex is interesting. While she indulged in
none of the now current vogue of explicit description, her
realistic attitude toward sex and marriage contributes markedly
to her effective handling of her central theme. She withstood
all temptation to pass moral judgment on Cicily and Albert
which results in the creation of two very convincing, incisive,
and three-dimensional portraits.[3]

In *Wisdom's Gate,* as in all her fiction, Mrs. Barnes made
clever use of minor figures to provide nuances in personality
and social background. Cicily's keen judgment of character is
shown by her mental view of the people at a family luncheon
at her mother-in-law's fashionable Lake Shore Drive apartment
soon after she and Albert have returned to Chicago:

Aunt Muriel, of course, had no intellectual interests whatever
and perhaps had been preserved by the calm that state engenders.
She seemed to Cicily to have grown no older and no less beautiful,
though quite a little heavier in the last five years. Her mature,
broad-bosomed figure was still impressively fashionable, cleverly
buttressed in her smart, dark gown. Her face was a triumph of the
very best cosmetics; her black hair was bobbed, thick, black, and
curly, with one white Whistler lock in it—perhaps the rest had been
touched up—and her bright blue eyes, clouded by lashes that certainly had been, looked joyous and youthful.

Her husband Ed Brown . . . a thick-set man, dark-haired in his
middle sixties, he had the smooth, indeterminate features of the
native Mid-Westerner and the non-committal expression of the
American business man, his jowl determined, his large nose pudgy,
his dark eyes jovial, though behind the joviality they gave nothing
away. He paused for an instant by Cicily's father . . . and Cicily
reflected that they made an odd pair.

Tall, spare, blue-eyed, and mildly reserved in manner, Stephen
Carver looked every inch a New Englander. Not at all like a banker,
Cicily decided—though he was a good one—like something much
less worldly. He had lost the brisk look of the busy executive that
had marked his middle years. Grown thinner, too, and greyer and
quite a little balder; and the baldness accenting the height of his
intellectual forehead gave him an innocent expression which Cicily
knew was slightly misleading. Success sat upon him less obviously
than it did on Ed Brown, conferring upon him no more than a quiet

air of authority. It had nothing to do with the distinction of his appearance, which was bred in his long, lean bones.

Ed Brown had no distinction; but you felt that success, the jade, had brought him his spruce black cutaway, his grey-striped trousers and the platinum watch-chain on his rotund waistcoat, and the silver [cocktail] shaker in his hand. His possessions and provisions, his Lake Shore Drive apartment and the entertainment he offered in it, were all the gifts of Success. So was Aunt Muriel, ripely seductive, who had consented at fifty to be Mrs. Ed Brown. (39–40)

Again, as in her other fiction, Margaret Barnes in *Wisdom's Gate* used décor effectively to give insight into her characters' attitudes and backgrounds. She introduced Jane and Stephen Carver and their family by a description of their living room:

The room . . . was somewhat old-fashioned, chintz-hung, book-lined, furnished with a few old pieces of mahogany furniture, a piano in the corner, an armchair and a sofa drawn close to the hearth. The clear country sunshine proclaimed it to be suburban and so did the view which the south and western windows commanded—a wide, unbroken stretch of flat, tanned fields. It was essentially a family room, suggesting in its atmosphere of comfortable domesticity that children had grown up in it; in its order that those children had left it. The impression was confirmed by the three framed photographs—the only ones in evidence—which stood on the piano, so placed that they could "keep company" with anyone who chanced to be sitting alone by the fire. Two fair-haired girls, one pretty and one plain, in what seemed like their late twenties, and a blond young man who looked younger. On a table by the armchair lay a pipe and a tobacco jar, a copy of *The Nation* and one of *The Atlantic Monthly*, and a book with a bookmark in it, James Truslow Adams' *The Epic of America*; on another by the sofa was a work bag of knitting. (3–4)

Mrs. Barnes developed well the shades of difference concerning codes of morality between the generation of Jane and that of Cicily. When Cicily questions her mother about the reputation of her late father-in-law Bert Lancaster whom she remembers only vaguely as an elderly invalid, Jane replies that he was considered a great beau. When Cicily then pursues the question of married women and beaux during the 1890's, Jane answers:

"They didn't have any [beaux]."

"Oh, Mumsy—"

"Well, we never heard about them."

"Never?"

"Hardly ever."

"Mumsy, what did you hear?"

"Very little, dear. Honestly. People weren't so articulate."

"But still, you knew—"

"We didn't know anything. We just sensed—occasionally—that there were things that—well, we ought to disapprove of."

Cicily's eyes were gleaming with amusement. "What things? Adultery?"

"We never heard that word spoken except by a vested clergyman." Jane was not shocked, but she was emphatic.

"But you knew what it meant?"

"No, we didn't—exactly."

"But still you disapproved of it?" Cicily smiled.

"Adultery," said Jane, pronouncing the word with great delibera- tion to show that she wasn't in the least afraid of it, "was not a— thing we ever thought of as actually happening."

"But yet you disapproved of those married women? The ones who had beaux, I mean?"

"Everyone did, dear. But there were very few of them."

"And of their beaux, too?"

"Certainly. Not as much, perhaps," Jane added honestly. . . .

"Did people disapprove of Albert's father . . . before he married Aunt Muriel?"

Jane admitted with reluctance, "He was said to be somewhat fast."

"What a wonderful word! Who was she, Mumsy?"

"I'm not going to tell you."[4]

"Did you know her?"

"Very well."

"Was she horrid?"

"No. She was lovely."

"Why, Mumsy, darling—how broad-minded of you. . . . Did Aunt Muriel know?"

"I think she did."

"Did it give her pause for thought?"

Jane shook her head.

"Well, I rather like that." Though Cicily's tone was a trifle un- certain, "It's honest and it's modern. What happened to the woman?"

In the pause that followed, Jane looked at her daughter so gravely that Cicily knew that she had sounded cavalier. Then, "She died," said Jane, very quietly.

"Then and there? Why, Mumsy—how romantic! Of a broken heart, you mean? Those were the days—" But then she observed that her casual reaction was jarring on her mother. It had jarred her to the point where she felt she must do something about it, say something serious to impress on her daughter the solemnity of this story, which seemed so remote, archaic, artificial, a fantasy of the 'nineties!

"She killed herself. . . ."

"Mumsy—she *didn't*!" Cicily was shocked out of modern objectivity. "How simply appalling. . . . What did Albert's father do?"

"Nothing."

"But he *must* have—"

"What could he do?"

"Gosh, I don't know. Where was he?"

"Away on his honeymoon."

"Golly!" said Cicily. The word spoke volumes. (117–20)

Wisdom's Gate, then, for the most part, deals with ideas recurrent in all of the fiction of Margaret Barnes. However, Mrs. Barnes developed one new theme: a discussion of suburban life. While she had touched upon the topic in *Years of Grace* and in *Within This Present*, she did not make it a subject of major concentration until the last novel where she developed her concepts with subtle skill.[5] Soon after Cicily and Albert's return to Chicago, they discuss with amusement the impending Thanksgiving luncheon, their first formal function where they will encounter all of their family for the first time since their divorce and remarriage. Cicily notices that Albert's attention has drifted; he is staring moodily out of the window of her parents' house at the landscape in the foreground:

Moreover, she knew what he saw. Suburban emptiness. The morning sunlight. The drive neatly raked and the bright red barberry bushes and the bare-boughed oak trees with a few brown leaves clinging to them. . . .

She reminded him, as if it mattered, "The view's on the other side of the house."

"The view!" he laughed shortly.

The residents of Lakewood always called the flat fields that. You could hardly acquiesce on coming back from China. Still, they offered a wider and more agreeable prospect than the vista the guestroom windows commanded, beyond the bare lawn, of the oddly

assorted houses of the three nearest neighbours. They were curiously
lacking in architectural unity. One Georgian red brick, one rustic
Italian stucco, one long flat bungalow of Frank Lloyd Wright design,
they stretched in a straight line along the unimposing ridge starkly
exposing their west fronts toward the fields, in wide, level "grounds"
that looked treeless in November.

"I hate Suburbia," said Albert presently. Then, "The Middle-
West's a funny place," as detached as if he hadn't been born in it.
"I'd like to take a train to the world's end, right after Mother's
luncheon."

"Why not before?" grinned Cicily, her thoughts comically recalled
to her the immediate ordeal. But when he turned around, he looked
so cast-down that she knew the comedy was misplaced.

"I'm sorry, Albert." She met and held his eyes, her own softening
with sympathy. What she was sorry about was the incontrovertible
fact that Albert's best chance of making money—indeed his only
one—lay here with the family, where he had always been known.

"Crude—rich—obvious—imitative—no atmosphere—no beauty—no imagination—no resources," he said deliberately. "Remote from everything—so, no escaping."

This seemed to sum it. She agreed with much of it. But still—
there was the safety. (35–37)

The safety that Cicily envisions is only partially the promise
of financial security. Equally she interprets it from an emotional
and psychological point of view which results from the
immutable social laws and belief in the sacrosanctity of the
marriage vows held by suburbia. This view is reinforced at her
first dinner party. Cicily, after her six years' experience in
international society

. . . felt a trifle remote from the jokes and anecdotes that she
heard all around her, though they were the sort of thing to which
she had listened at every Lakewood party only six years ago. Women
talked of their children and gossiped of their neighbours and men
discussed business in the cracks of conversation left by their voluble
wives. The men, in particular, seemed uninteresting and uninterested.
They displayed an indifference to Cicily's effort—for she had learned
in the Legation always to exert one—to entertain and charm them.
She missed a certain quality, not important but stimulating, which
candour compelled her to define as appreciation. But then, she
remembered, she couldn't have it both ways. . . . They're married
and that's ended it. Or at least that's the assumption. I wonder if

it's true. Do they all love their wives or have they dismissed dalliance because they're tired and busy and preoccupied with money-making, and in the social pattern here it's really impractical? But at this point she realized, somewhat to her surprise, that she was thinking like a decadent European and casting a shadow of doubt on the safety of Lakewood. She made an honest effort to listen more attentively to the conversation of the women, who were earnestly discussing how they could keep the children's Christmas parties simpler than they'd been last year. (82–83)

Yet, as Cicily learns, masculine indifference turns the cultivated sophistication of a man like Albert into very heady wine for the feminine society. Also, she discovers that, the more immutable the social laws, the more daring the transgressor appears. The fascination of a woman like Gertrude Sewall springs largely from the simple fact that she ignores the set standards of social behavior. When she directly telephones Albert at his office to invite him to dinner, Cicily becomes enraged because Gertrude flagrantly violates the suburban commandment which decreed that the hostess must ask the wife if she might "borrow" her husband to even the number at the party. Albert complains that Cicily's rigid adherence to the established code is another example of her romantic philosophy. Romanticism, he insists, is what makes American suburbia so unpalatable. On the one hand, the romantic transforms the landscape into a repetitive, imitative line of Georgian mansions and Italian villas, while, on the other hand, he draws a bleak, unimaginative design for living. Albert tells Cicily:

"Your romanticism . . . is your one puritanical streak. A craving for perfection is essentially romantic. It was merely romanticism that made the Puritans' Blue Laws and tied libertines to whipping posts and put harlots in stocks. They were far too romantic to live and let live, take life as it comes and accept human nature for what it must be. They made a lot of trouble, for themselves and other people, by what they saw and wouldn't see—." (35)

Although *Wisdom's Gate* is interesting, there is no escape from the reaction that the novel is anticlimactic after *Years of Grace, Within This Present,* and *Edna His Wife.* Perhaps the most disappointing factor about it is that it should have been Mrs. Barnes's last work. When she had preceded it by such fine studies in social history, it does seem too bad that she should have ended her literary career on a minor note.

CHAPTER 8

The Summing Up

A N APPRAISAL of Margaret Ayer Barnes's total performance poses significant problems. The range of her fiction appears extremely narrow especially when compared with the work of other twentieth-century American novelists of manners like Edith Wharton, F. Scott Fitzgerald, or John O'Hara. She wrote almost exclusively about the American upper middle class; so, unlike Mrs. Wharton, she produced no comparative studies of American and European society. Also she seldom took her characters out of their milieu, which meant that, unlike Fitzgerald or O'Hara, she was not concerned with contrasting the differences in outlook that developed among the social classes in America. Although she largely chose Chicago for her setting, she was never a regional novelist.

Mrs. Barnes's interest was in the study of the upper middle class as a whole, not as it evolved in the Middle West; her drawing rooms could have been found in any American city. As a result, she never displayed the particularism of O'Hara which led to his artful analysis of the contrasts in the society of the Philadelphia Main Line with that of Long Island. Mrs. Barnes's confined scope did not allow for great diversity either in subject matter or in characterization.[1] As one critic has noted: "She has movement and suspense. But she subjects her characters to technique. Her people are human but are not markedly individualized problems. They are era people and group people."[2]

Her desire to produce social history caused her in many instances to use her characters as personifications of ideas or as attitudes of the particular period about which she was writing. Although she presented astute psychological interpretations of her characters, she did not explore deeply the realm of their inner life. She analyzed in depth their consciousness rather than their subconsciousness, which perhaps has made some critics feel that she never more than superficially skimmed the surface of human existence.[3] If her work reflects no Freudian influence, a close study of Margaret Barnes's fiction shows that she was very much aware of the tense conflict between human desires and social mores. Although her characters do flaunt conventional social standards, they scarcely rank as social radicals, which may account for the current critical view of her as a staunch conservative. But she demonstrated clearly that she believed that social conformity never led to a total satisfaction or complete happiness; at best, she thought it brought "peace without victory."[4]

Similarly, she painted her portrait of the American scene as she saw it. She was concerned with the actual and the real, not with the ideal and the ultimate, which certainly restricted her development as a creative artist. No one would argue that the successful chronicler, who must "tell it as it is" and detail it carefully as he sees it, must check his creative imagination.

Nevertheless, within her chosen, restricted domain, Mrs. Barnes re-created finely that social milieu. If she wrote exclusively about the life she lived, much more important was the fact that she had analyzed thoroughly what she considered the strength and the foibles of that life before she began to write. Thus her presentation, like Edith Wharton's, has authenticity and authority. Furthermore, her style is "as effortless and right as the style of the lady who dresses well by instinct."[5] Her dialogue never fails to achieve a lifelike quality. Her objectivity and sense of empathy buttress even the most superficial characterizations and trivial situations with underpinnings of realism.

To Mrs. Barnes, the essential goal of fiction was to capture the vital spirit of history; and the accomplishment of that purpose required the author to adopt a definite frame of reference: "The average reader likes to perceive in the pattern of a plot the shadowy design of his own personal problems. And one thing is certain—that men and women in every age believe some things to be good and others to be bad, and try with indifferent success in the perplexity of living, to differentiate between them.

It is the task of the writer to interpret that effort to portray
the heliotropic struggle of humanity in the jungle of existence
to reach the sun."[6] Therefore, Margaret Barnes judged the social
purpose of literature to be as essential as the artistic aim.
Specifically, the task of the American author, she felt, should
be to record the voices of opinion and the patterns of thought
extant in America with precision and artistry.[7] Fiction written
from this perspective would produce dynamic, historical interpretations of the past which would illuminate new goals for
American democracy to pursue.

Twentieth-century America, she continued, must apply the
same zealous pioneer spirit toward the conquest of the social
frontier that nineteenth-century America had employed to conquer the physical frontier.[8] She believed the achievement of this
objective hinged upon the development of a new feminism and
the revitalization of the leadership of the upper middle class.
In this respect, the critic must never forget, when considering
Mrs. Barnes's point of view, that she grew up in the Chicago
of Jane Addams and in the Illinois of John Peter Altgeld. She
saw that social progress grew from inspired service rendered
by the upper middle class American; for wealth and position
did not dim the social conscience of persons like Louise deKoven
Bowen, Anita McCormick Blaine, Henry Demerest Lloyd, or
Lyman J. Gage. She never lost her faith in the belief that
cooperative leadership could revitalize a nation disillusioned
by war and scarred by depression. As may be easily seen, her
fiction anticipates and closely parallels current social historical
studies like Betty Friedan's *The Feminine Mystique* and E.
Digby Baltzell's *The Protestant Establishment*.

Considering Mrs. Barnes's Chicago background and her Bryn
Mawr legacy, it would have been strange if the importance of
feminism had not constituted a dominant theme running through
the whole body of her fiction. Mrs. Friedan's recognition of
woman's "identity crisis" was a common subject in Mrs. Barnes's
novels: "The search for identity of the young man who can't
go home again has always been a major theme of American
writers. And it has always been considered right in America,
good, for men to suffer these agonies of growth, to search for
and find their own identities. . . . But why have theorists not
recognized this same identity crisis in women?"[8]

In treating the feminine quest for identity, Mrs. Barnes portrayed astutely the dilemma of the college-trained woman, like Martha Cavendish or Jane Carver, in reconciling the aspirations acquired by higher education with the traditional female role. She showed equally acute insight in her analysis of the predicament of the untrained wife of the drivingly ambitious, self-made businessman like that of Edna Jones. In every instance Mrs. Barnes underscored the fact that marriage and motherhood alone do not bring fulfillment; the woman must face the challenge of alienation directly before she can gain an understanding of herself as an individual. Furthermore, she stressed that no woman can contribute substantially either to marriage or to the home without having achieved a sense of vocation.

The tang of *Westward Passage* that removes it from the category of "slick fiction" comes from Margaret Barnes's recognition of the desperation of a woman like Olivia Ottendorf. At first glance, perhaps any problem of a lovely, spoiled, wealthy woman who behaves like an irresponsible adolescent may appear ridiculously inconsequential. But Mrs. Barnes saw her as a social calamity, for Olivia's training and education prepared her only to make a socially advantageous marriage. She rebels because she wants to do something more with her life; but she lacks the background to accomplish anything else. Only when she comes to grips realistically with herself and accepts the conventional society which she graces so elegantly does she attain something of the feeling of being an individual. However, she remains a stunted individual; for whatever ability she may have possessed inherently has been sacrificed to the cult of "genteel" femininity.

Margaret Barnes suggested that the traditional nineteenth-century concept of the married woman causes social waste, for she never uses her talent to the fullest. She develops, like so many of Mrs. Barnes's heroines, into an extremely incisive person; but she seldom employs her knowledge to solve issues outside of the small circle of family and intimate friends. If Mrs. Barnes felt the married woman could come to terms with herself and even discover a vocation in the harmonization of personal interests with domestic demands, she drew a grim picture of the plight of the spinster. Jane Carver pronounces: "What families did to single women. Well-to-do families, throwing destitute middle-aged daughters an occasional diamond horse shoe, but denying them the right to independence. The right to life, liberty, and the pursuit of happiness."[9]

The life of Flora Furness, Jane Carver's close friend, graphically illustrates this opinion. Flora, from the moment of her mother's suicide at the end of her debut year, is victimized by her demanding, bereaved father. At thirty-seven,

> Her red gold hair was just as shiny as ever, her figure was as slender and eyes as brightly blue. She had never lost that look of the Dresden-china shepherdess. Was it just because Flora had never really done anything that she still seemed as delicate and fragile and fair as a precious piece of porcelain? Things had always been done *to* Flora. From the hour of her mother's dreadful, dishonored death, her life had been swallowed up by her aging father. He had carried her around an empty world, trying to fill its emptiness with her Dresden-china prettiness. She had summered in England and France and Germany and Switzerland. She had wintered in Italy and Egypt and India and Spain. She had opened and closed the brown-stone house on Rush Street for innumerable Chicago seasons. But she had never settled down, never really belonged anywhere.[10]

When Margaret Barnes shifted her analysis of social attitudes about the status of women from the nineteenth to the twentieth century, she detected shrewd differences in the feminine outlook. Young women, like Cicily Lancaster and Sally McLeod who are caught in the emotional whirlpool of World War I, are thoroughly unprepared to cope with the realities of marriage; nevertheless, they possess a spirit of decisiveness that enables them to face their difficulties squarely rather than to sublimate them. They act, and, through their action, they gain emotional maturity, if not security. They view life as a ceaseless adventure, and they accept the uncertainty about their future as an integral part of that adventure.

Mrs. Barnes also depicted the spirit of determination for self-development in the unmarried woman. Jenny Carver and Cora Truesdale, unlike Flora Furness, chafe against family impositions. They seize the first opportunity to assert their independence and to grow as individuals as a result of their choice. The case of Cora Truesdale is particularly interesting, because she represents the example of the self-made woman.

Cora, whose formal education consists only of the traditional boarding school, wins a prized position on the staff of *The New Yorker* through her determination to develop her natural literary gift so that she can compete with persons who have the academic credentials and the professional experience that she totally lacks.

Perhaps the characterization of Jean Howland best expresses Margaret Barnes's attitude about the feminine role. Jean, Vassar graduate, Hull House resident, and doctoral candidate at the University of Chicago, can offer both intellectual and emotional stimulus to Georgie Truesdale. These two experience a great sense of self-fulfillment, as well as a strengthening of their personal relationship, in their service together doing relief work during the critical years of the early New Deal.

While Mrs. Barnes devoted a great deal of her fiction to the examination of modern feminism, she allotted equal discussion to the reasons for the decline of the dynamism in the leadership of the upper middle class American in the twentieth century. Professor Baltzell in *The Protestant Establishment* summarized her view when he wrote: "A crisis in moral authority has developed in modern America largely because of the White-Anglo-Saxon-Protestant establishment's unwillingness, or inability, to share and improve its upper-class traditions by continuously absorbing talented and distinguished members of minority groups into its privileged ranks."[11]

Margaret Barnes portrayed this "upper-class establishment" as having, with almost calculated deliberation, withdrawn into a state of isolation from the ideas and issues of their time. Every member of the Sewall family reflects the background of education, culture, and a wide variety of interests. Although aware of the social and economic problems of their day, not one of them cares sufficiently about these questions to break from his or her well-bred little world to provide the active leadership which by heritage and training they are well equipped to do. They steel themselves against the encroachment of any outsiders and almost to a man oppose Kathleen Truesdale's marriage to Maurice Edelstein on the basis of his Lower East Side New York, Jewish birthright.

A basic cause for this complacent unconcern and stubborn prejudice, Margaret Barnes proposed, grew from   the failure

of American higher education. The majority of her masculine
characters are graduates of the prestigious eastern colleges. Yet
none shows the remotest awareness about issues outside of the
business world or about any idea not currently discussed at the
country club. Some of the younger generation do express dissatisfaction about the existing educational system; for, when Alan
McLeod, a Harvard senior, enlists upon the American declaration of war in 1917, he explains to Sally Sewall that he wants
to fight because he believes a new social order can arise despite
the slaughter and devastation. When she questions whether any
enlightened society can be given birth through militarism, Alan
retorts: " 'At any rate, I know they're [new social orders] not
made in colleges. At least they're not made there by boys like
. . . me. What am I studying at Harvard? Economics 24, Banking
3, and Elementary Spanish. Dad says Spanish is useful to a
banker because of South America. He sees a future for me selling
Peruvian bonds! Now, Sally, you know that's bunk. Harvard's
a pleasant club . . . and I enjoy it. Meanwhile the world is burning up.' "[12] The most four years at Harvard gives to Steve Carver
is a love of Boston and the Beacon Hill tradition. Paul Jones, Jr.,
regrets his failure simply because he likes the convivial atmosphere of Cambridge.

Similarly, Michael in "Arms and the Boy," despite his experiences in World War I, demonstrates no intellectual curiosity
when he returns to Princeton. The problems of the postwar world
never occupy his thought, although he has seen firsthand their
development. He receives his degree; but a college education
means to him primarily Princeton-Yale football games and New
York weekends. Neither World War I nor Princeton stirs Michael
to do anything more than to forget both experiences as soon
as possible.

Mrs. Barnes viewed the professional man, too, as displaying
only patent disinterest about current issues. Chuck Dayton and
Lambert Sewall as Episcopal clergymen have the opportunity to
stimulate the social consciences of their wealthy congregations.
Dayton uses the pulpit to parade his good looks and charm
before an admiring public. Sewall's thoughts evolve in glittering,
safe platitudes or become violently jingoist, as in his pro-Allied
sermons, when he feels the occasion demands it. Matthew
Martin does brilliant, original work in cancer research and has

the means as the director of the Pierrepont Institute to make significant contributions to humanity; yet he seeks the position solely to fan the flames of his ego.

If Margaret Barnes depicted the moral stagnation of the upper middle class Americans, she portrayed also their moral strength. She considered the impact of World War I so shook the foundations of their society that never again were they fully able to retreat into the social exclusiveness of the prewar decade. The spirit of the leadership that emerged in Washington during the war illustrates graphically that in a period of critical emergency the upper middle class not only serves selflessly but, perhaps more important, recognizes the need to advance the course of democracy. The circle over which the wealthy, aristocratic Viola and Arthur Sloane preside includes dedicated men and women of varied backgrounds and climates of opinion. All of these people work diligently and effectively to implement programs that will assist in democratizing the postwar world.

However, once the danger and the excitement of the war ends, the spirit of service as a universal force disintegrates but does not disappear. The Arthur Sloanes, when they resume their life in New York, gather at their dinner parties people similar in outlook to those whom they have known in Washington. Their salon forms the setting for a lively interchange of divergent viewpoints about contemporary questions; but, since these people are not just attractive dilettantes but are involved in civic affairs, their discussions do form the basis for social action. Furthermore, Mrs. Barnes believed the actual experience in the horror of the war awakened in many men and women an awareness of humanitarianism they had never known previously. Fred Sewall's experience as an ambulance driver changes him from a handsome playboy into a man who searches for ways to contribute to human betterment. Rose McLeod's work with the Red Cross in France transforms her from a lovely, sheltered debutante into a woman painfully aware of the tragedy of the human plight. Georgie Truesdale at Harvard during the postwar years derives a very genuine desire to serve humanity. Mrs. Barnes emphasized through these individual examples that the reform impulse did survive the decade of the 1920's. However, she also held that the progressive loss of idealism demonstrated by the attitude of the majority of the upper middle class during that same era made that group partly responsible for the revolutionary temper stimulated by the Great Depression.

Margaret Barnes believed that the Great Depression could accomplish what the Great War had failed to effect—the revitalization of the democratic process; and the New Deal program and the leadership of Franklin Roosevelt promised that fulfillment. As has been seen, when the Sewall family listened to Roosevelt's first inaugural address, the members, regardless of generation, thrilled to its challenge; all felt a special obligation to act—to participate in the rehabilitation of America. They understand that the survival of the democratic tradition hinges upon their ability to extend the advantages they have regarded as exclusively their own to all segments of society. Mrs. Barnes saw in the early New Deal response to the catastrophe of the Great Depression the human incentive to push beyond the existing social frontier provided that the established leadership continued to move forward from this auspicious beginning. If she took an optimistic view about the future of America, it was not one of blind optimism.

The fiction of Margaret Ayer Barnes has not attracted much attention from contemporary literary historians. One primary reason for this somewhat cursory dismissal is that she is a thoroughly conventional novelist in an era of fictional experimentation. But it does not follow that her work is inferior to that of the experimentalist. If she speaks with gentility, she speaks also with authority and dispassionate objectivity. At her best, she combines the psychological insight and depth of character analysis of the experimentalist with the ability to produce a satisfying narrative of the traditionalist.[13]

One critic recently included *Years of Grace* among the fifty novels so far written in this century that he believed would always provide an interesting, provocative literary experience.[14] This judgment could apply to all of her major novels and to parts of her minor ones. For the student of American social history, the fiction of Margaret Ayer Barnes will remain a limited but an important record.

Notes and References

Preface

1. Robert E. Spiller *et al.*, eds., *The Literary History of the United States* (New York, 1966), p. 319.
2. Max J. Herzberg, *The Reader's Encyclopedia of American Literature* (New York, 1961), p. 61.
3. William J. Stuckey, *The Pulitzer Prize Novels: A Critical Backward Look* (Norman, Oklahoma, 1966), p. 89.
4. For Mrs. Barnes's evaluation of Franklin Roosevelt and the early New Deal, see her novel *Within This Present* (Boston, 1933), pp. 605–11.
5. Herbert R. Mayes, "Trade Winds," *Saturday Review* (April 6, 1968), 10.
6. F. P. Barach, *Books* (November 18, 1933), 29.
7. "Period Novel," *What Is a Book*, ed. Dale Warren (Boston, 1935), p. 214.

Chapter One

1. Eric Wollencott Barnes, *The Man Who Lived Twice: The Biography of Edward Sheldon* (New York, 1936), p. 20.
2. "Margaret Ayer Barnes," *Twentieth Century Authors*, ed. Stanley Kaunitz (New York, 1942), p. 78.
3. Alice Martin Hawkins, *Bryn Mawr Alumnae Bulletin* (Winter, 1968).
4. "Margaret Ayer Barnes Folder," New York Public Library Annex, New York, New York.
5. The Board of Directors of Bryn Mawr did not retain records of their meetings at this time, so it is impossible to describe except in a general way the work of Margaret Barnes in the project.
6. Hilda Worthington Smith, "Bryan Mawr Summer School for Women Workers in Industry," *Proceedings and Addresses of the National Education Association* LX (1922), 713–14. The school ran under Miss Smith's direction from 1921 until 1934, and it inspired the initiation of similar programs at Barnard (1927–34), the Vineyard Shore School for Women Workers in Industry (1929–34), and the Brookwood Labor College. Professor Clarke A. Chambers wrote:

"The significance of the Bryn Mawr School for Working Women and similar programs . . . is difficult to measure. It is fair to suggest, however, that they kept alive a commitment to trade union activity; they trained young men and women who were to become union and political leaders of some note during the depression decade; they kindled the aspirations of many young people in time of moral slump; they kept open the path of purposeful social change." *Seedtime of Reform* (Minneapolis, 1963), pp. 80–81.

7. Anon., New York *Sun*, October 31, 1933.

8. Margaret Ayer Barnes, "Address," New York League of Advertising Women, New York *Times*, February 10, 1932.

9. *Man Who Lived Twice*, p. 151.

10. Quoted in *Man Who Lived Twice*, p. 152.

11. Quoted in *Man Who Lived Twice*, p. 156.

12. Anon., Section 9, New York *Times*, February 10, 1929; *Man Who Lived Twice*, p. 154.

13. Quoted in *Man Who Lived Twice*, pp. 154–55.

14. Percy Hammond, New York *Herald Tribune*, *Age of Innocence Notebook*, Katherine Cornell-Guthrie McClintic Manuscripts Collection, Theater Collection at Lincoln Center, New York Public Library, New York, New York.

15. St. John Ervin, New York *World*; John Anderson; Rowland Field, *Age of Innocence Notebook*.

16. *Man Who Lived Twice*, p. 283.

17. *Ibid.*, p. 207.

18. *Westward Passage* (Boston, 1931).

Chapter Two

1. Preface, *Prevailing Winds* (Boston, 1932), p. xiii.

2. The other stories in the collection are "Home Fire," "Set a Thief," "Shirtsleeves to Shirtsleeves," and "The Eyes of Youth." While they are all clever and amusing, they have little relevance to the thesis of this study. Perhaps the most entertaining is "Set a Thief." It centers on the scheme devised by a young woman, who aspires to be a playwright, that enables her to write the sensational drama of a New York season. She lures a famous but insufferably conceited dramatist into believing she will have an affair with him because he has achieved his fame by dramatizing in a very transparent fashion his affairs with prominent socialites and actresses. Once she gains the information she needs, she breaks with him; and he has the ignominious experience of seeing himself become the subject of the most popular and the most critically acclaimed comedy of the season.

3. *Prevailing Winds* (Boston, 1928), p. 57. All succeeding page references are to this edition. Page numbers follow quotations.

4. Preface, *ibid.*, xiii-xiv.

5. Anon., *Saturday Review of Literature*, V (November 10, 1928), 358; Anon., New York *Times Book Review*, November 25, 1928.

Chapter Three

1. *Years of Grace* (Boston, 1930), p. 42. All succeeding page references are to this edition. Page numbers follow quotations.

2. Proteus, *New Statesman*, XXXV (August 16, 1930), 596.

3. Anon., New York *Times Book Review*, July 6, 1930; Robert M. Lovett, *New Republic*, LXIII (July 23, 1930), 298; Dorothy Van Doren, *Nation*, CXXX (August 6, 1930), 158; Anon., London *Times Literary Supplement*, October 9, 1930.

4. Quoted in New York *Times*, November 18, 1936.

5. *Ibid.*

6. Professor Commager considered in *The American Mind* (New Haven, 1950), p. 41: "The decade of the nineties is the watershed of American history. As with all watersheds the topography is blurred, but in the perspective of half a century the grand outlines emerge clearly. On the one side lies an America predominantly agricultural; concerned with domestic problems; conforming intellectually at least, to the political, economic, and moral principles inherited from the seventeenth and eighteenth centuries; an America on the whole self-confident, self-contained, self-reliant, and conscious of its unique character and of a unique destiny. On the other side lies the modern America, predominantly urban and industrial; inextricably involved in world economy and politics; troubled with problems that had long been thought peculiar to the Old World; experiencing profound changes in population, social institutions, economy, and technology; and trying to accommodate its traditional institutions and habits of thought to conditions new and in part alien."

7. Anon., New York *Times Book Review*.

8. Proteus, *New Statesman*.

When *Years of Grace* won the Pulitzer Prize in 1931, it led to a critical reprise of the novel. The general consensus was that, while it was a worthwhile work that should have been written and deserved its popularity, it was not the best novel published during 1930. Of course, to single out one novel as the best written in any year is bound to provoke controversy; moreover, the secrecy of the selection of the Pulitzer committee and the refusal to permit inspection of the committee reports contributed markedly to the dissension. During the early decades of the award in the 1920's and the 1930's, the selected novel particularly seemed to provoke a critical storm. As the years have passed, the furor has abated somewhat due in part to more awards and in part to the resignation of the reviewers to the conservatism of the committee.

In 1930, when the possible selections included William Faulkner's *As I Lay Dying,* John Dos Passos' *Forty Second Parallel,* and Elizabeth Madox Roberts' *The Great Meadow,* the question definitely would arise as to whether a neophyte like Margaret Ayer Barnes would be capable of writing a novel which could match the artistry of these serious, more experienced authors. If time is a valid critical yardstick, the fiction of Miss Roberts, Dos Passos, and Faulkner has received acclaim and that of Mrs. Barnes has passed into oblivion. However, in the final analysis, the value and importance of any creative work rests largely upon personal opinion.

Perhaps there is one factor about the attitudes of the Pulitzer juries that has been overlooked: the modernity of their judgment from the current academic point of view. The emphasis today on interdisciplinary studies is very similar to the novels selected to receive the Pulitzer Prize.

In almost every instance the authors who received the Pulitzer Prize used fiction as the medium to examine and to explain the development of American social, economic, and political attitudes.

Chapter Four

1. *Westward Passage* (Boston, 1931), p. 4. All succeeding page references are to this edition. Page numbers follow quotations.

2. Margaret Lawrence, *The School of Femininity* (New York, 1936), p. 225.

3. Virgilia Peterson Ross, *Outlook and Independent,* CLIX (December 9, 1931), 473–74); *New Republic,* LXIX (January 6, 1932), 224; Ethel Wallace Hawkins, *Atlantic Monthly,* CXLIX (February, 1932), 18.

4. "Margaret Ayer Barnes Folder," New York Public Library Annex, New York, New York.

5. *New Republic.*

6. Virgilia Peterson Ross, *Outlook and Independent.*

7. Ethel Wallace Hawkins, *Atlantic Monthly.*

Chapter Five

1. While Mrs. Barnes was completing *Within This Present,* Henry Kitchell Webster, the popular Chicago novelist and lifelong friend of the Ayer family, died on December 9, 1932. He left an unfinished

manuscript *The Alleged Great-Aunt,* a rather pedestrian mystery novel. As an act of friendship, Margaret Barnes and Janet Ayer Fairbank decided to collaborate on preparing the manuscript for publication. However, they ended by turning their collaboration into "an experiment in imitative writing." "The point where the collaboration began is our little mystery," they explained in their preface. Although *The Alleged Great-Aunt* is decidedly mediocre, the collaboration of Mrs. Barnes and Mrs. Fairbank would have to be considered a success because no one was able to detect the slightest stylistic change. See "Henry Kitchell Webster," *Twentieth Century Authors,* ed. Stanley J. Kunitz and Howard Haycraft (New York, 1942), p. 1487.

2. *Within This Present* (Boston, 1933), p. 35. All succeeding page references are to this edition. Page numbers follow quotations.

3. Hershell Brickell, "The Literary Landscaper," *North American Review,* CCXXXIV (January, 1934), 92–93.

4. Elizabeth Lyman Brown, New York *Times Book Review,* November 12, 1933.

5. Hershell Brickell, "The Literary Landscaper."

6. Gladys Graham, *Saturday Review of Literature,* X (November 11, 1933), 253.

Chapter Six

1. *Edna His Wife* (Boston, 1935), pp. 4–6. All succeeding page references are to this edition. Page numbers follow quotations.

2. Rebecca Lowrie, *Saturday Review of Literature,* XIII (November 8, 1935), 7.

3. Edith H. Walton, New York *Times Book Review,* November 10, 1935.

Chapter Seven

1. *Wisdom's Gate* (Boston, 1938), pp. 55–56. All succeeding page references are to this edition. Page numbers follow quotations.

2. Rebecca Lowrie, *Saturday Review of Literature,* XIX (November 5, 1938), 7; Louise Maunsell Field, New York *Times Book Review,* November 6, 1938.

3. Rebecca Lowrie, *Saturday Review of Literature.*

4. For a summary of Bert Lancaster's affair with Lily Furness, see Chapter Three.

5. Louise Maunsell Field, New York *Times Book Review.*

Chapter Eight

1. Basil Davenport, *Saturday Review of Literature,* VIII (December 5, 1931), 345.

2. Margaret Lawrence, *The School of Femininity*, p. 225.

3. Basil Davenport, *Saturday Review of Literature*.

4. Margaret Ayer Barnes, "Perpetual Care," *Prevailing Winds*, p. 263.

5. Basil Davenport, *Saturday Review of Literature*.

6. "Period Novel," *What Is a Book*, ed. Dale Warren (Boston, 1935), pp. 218–19.

7. *Ibid.*, p. 214.

8. "The Town We Grew Up In," *Survey Graphic*, XXIII (October, 1934), 457.

9. Betty Friedan *The Feminine Mystique* (New York, 1963), pp. 78–79.

10. *Years of Grace* (Boston, 1930), p. 246.

11. *Ibid.*, pp. 282–83.

12. E. Digby Baltzell, *The Protestant Establishment* (New York, 1964), p. x.

13. Howard Mumford Jones and Richard M. Ludwig, *Guide to American Literature and Its Background Since 1890* (Cambridge, Massachusetts, 1964), p. 207. Professor Jones and Professor Ludwig wrote: "Not all writers of talent yielded to the mood of experimentation that characterized much fiction in the second quarter of the present century. Many were content to keep to the usual conventions of the novel, borrowing from the experimentalists the wider range of topics, deeper richness of psychological distrust of classifying human beings into types, while retaining some of the older concepts of novel writing, that fiction has the primary duty of story-telling and another duty of pleasing the intelligent reader. Literary histories are commonly unkind to novels of this sort, which in some other era, might have drawn to themselves a greater degree of critical attention. It is a mark of critical imperceptivity to assume, because a writer produces a 'conventional' novel, that he is therefore an inferior writer."

14. Herbert R. Mayes, "Trade Winds," *Saturday Review* (April 6, 1968), p. 10.

Selected Bibliography

PRIMARY SOURCES

1. Novels

Years of Grace. Boston: Houghton Mifflin Company, 1930.
Westward Passage. Boston: Houghton Mifflin Company, 1931.
Within This Present. Boston: Houghton Mifflin Company, 1933.
Edna His Wife. Boston: Houghton Mifflin Company, 1935.

2. Short Stories

Prevailing Winds. Boston: Houghton Mifflin Company, 1928. Reprinted in 1932 by Houghton Mifflin Company with Preface by Margaret Ayer Barnes. Includes "Feather Beds," "The Dinner Party," "Arms and the Boy," "Perpetual Care," "Home Fire," "Set a Thief," "Shirtsleeves to Shirtsleeves," and "The Eyes of Youth."

3. Essays

"The Town We Grew Up In," *Survey Graphic,* XXIII (October, 1934), 457.
"Period Novel," *What Is a Book.* Ed. Dale Warren. Boston: Houghton Mifflin Company, 1935.

SECONDARY SOURCES

1. Books

BARNES, ERIC WOLLENCOTT. *The Man Who Lived Twice: The Biography of Edward Sheldon.* New York: Charles Scribner, 1956. Contains helpful information about the youth of Margaret Ayer Barnes: invaluable source for the story of her automobile accident; the long illness and convalescence which resulted from it; the resumption of her friendship with Edward Sheldon which launched her literary career; their theatrical collaboration; her work as a playwright.

LAWRENCE, MARGARET. *The School of Femininity.* New York: Frederick G. Stokes, 1936. Reissued by Kennikat Press, Port Washington, New York, 1966. Contains the fullest critical study of Margaret Ayer Barnes.

STUCKEY, WILLIAM J. *The Pulitzer Prize Novels: A Critical Backward Look.* Norman, Okla.: The University of Oklahoma Press, 1966. Contains interesting but biased critical evaluation of *Years of Grace.* Intent is to debunk the methods of selection of the Pulitzer Prize novels and the novels generally which have won the Prize.

WAGENECHT, EDWARD. *Chicago.* Norman, Okla.: The University of Oklahoma Press, 1964. Very good source for the general background about Chicago; has interesting comments about the fiction of Margaret Ayer Barnes.

2. Reviews

These are especially important, since the work of Margaret Ayer Barnes has received such scanty reference in general critical studies and in literary histories.

Prevailing Winds

ANON. New York *Times Book Review,* November 25, 1928.
ANON. *Saturday Review of Literature,* V (November 10, 1928), 358.

Years of Grace

ANON. London *Times Literary Supplement,* October 9, 1930.
LOVETT, ROBERT M. *New Republic,* LXIII (July 23, 1930), 298.
New York *Times Book Review,* July 6, 1930.
Proteus. *New Statesman,* XXXV (August 16, 1930), 596.
VAN DOREN, DOROTHY. *Nation,* CXXX (August 6, 1930), 158.

Westward Passage

DAVENPORT, RUSSELL. *Saturday Review of Literature,* VIII (December 5, 1931), 345.
HAWKINS, ETHEL WALLACE. *Atlantic Monthly,* CXLIX (February, 1932), 18.
New Republic, LXIX (January 6, 1932), 224.
Ross, VIRGILIA PETERSON. *Outlook and Independent,* CLIX (December 9, 1931), 473–74.

Within This Present

BRICKELL, HERSHELL. "The Literary Landscaper," *North American Review* (January, 1934), 92–93.

BROWN, ELIZABETH LYMAN. New York *Times Book Review,* November 12, 1933.

GRAHAM, GLADYS. *Saturday Review of Literature,* X (November 11, 1933), 253.

Edna His Wife

LOWRIE, REBECCA. *Saturday Review of Literature,* XIII (November 9, 1935), 7.

WALTON, EDITH H. New York *Times Book Review,* November 10, 1935.

Wisdom's Gate

FIELD, LOUISE MAUNSELL. New York *Times Book Review,* November 6, 1938.

LOWRIE, REBECCA. *Saturday Review of Literature,* XIX (November 5, 1938), 7.

Index

149

In 1930 Margaret Ayer Barnes blazed meteorically across the American literary horizon with the publication of her first novel *Years of Grace,* which won her the Pulitzer Prize the following year. Like *Years of Grace,* each of her subsequent five novels when they first appeared usually found their way to the "best seller" and "recommended reading" lists. Unlike many popular authors, she consistently drew a favorable critical response. Nevertheless, in current literary histories one would be hard pressed to discover anything more than a fleeting reference to her or to her work.

The contemporary neglect of Mrs. Barnes is a fate which she shares generally with many other literary figures who have been dismissed because of the intense concentration on the great. However, few writers have presented such an exhaustive, dispassionate critique of the attitude and the way of life of the upper-middle-class American during those vital years of change from the Spanish-American War through the Great Depression. The basis for this full-length study of Margaret Ayer Barnes is, therefore, the belief that her fiction recreates vividly one segment of the social scene of late nineteenth- and early twentieth-century America. Her novels offer an invaluable source for the study of American social history.

The reputation of Margaret Ayer Barnes will rest more upon her accomplishment as a social historian rather than as a literary artist. This assessment does not suggest in any respect that she did not write fluent, lucid prose and was not an excellent narrator; but it does mean that she did not make any experimental contributions in style. The special talent of Mrs. Barnes lay in her ability to capture the spirit of the historical